Joseph Mills

Inner City

Essay by Anne Tucker

Nazraeli Press

HEMPHILL

Inner City

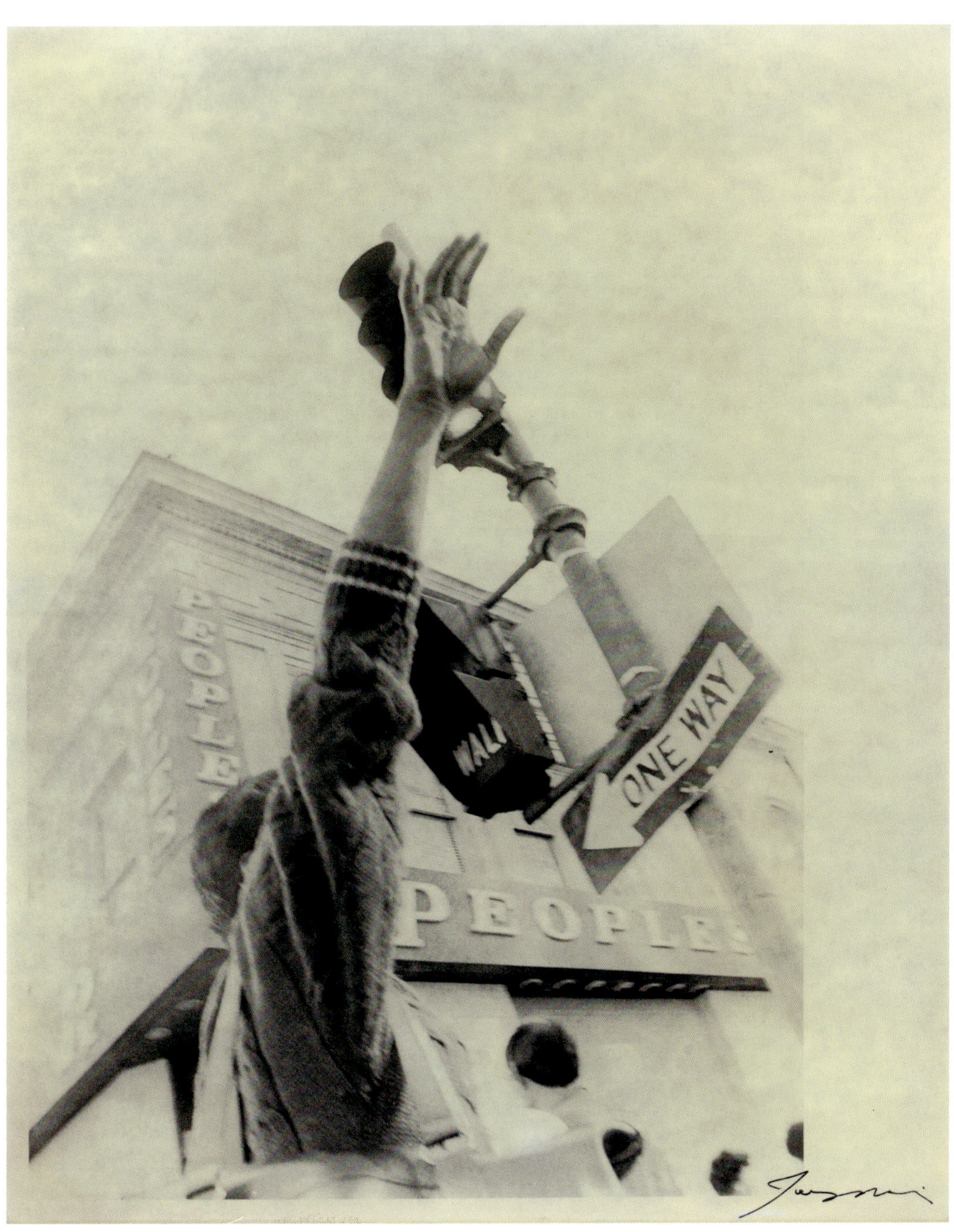
PEOPLE
PEOPLES
WALL
ONE WAY

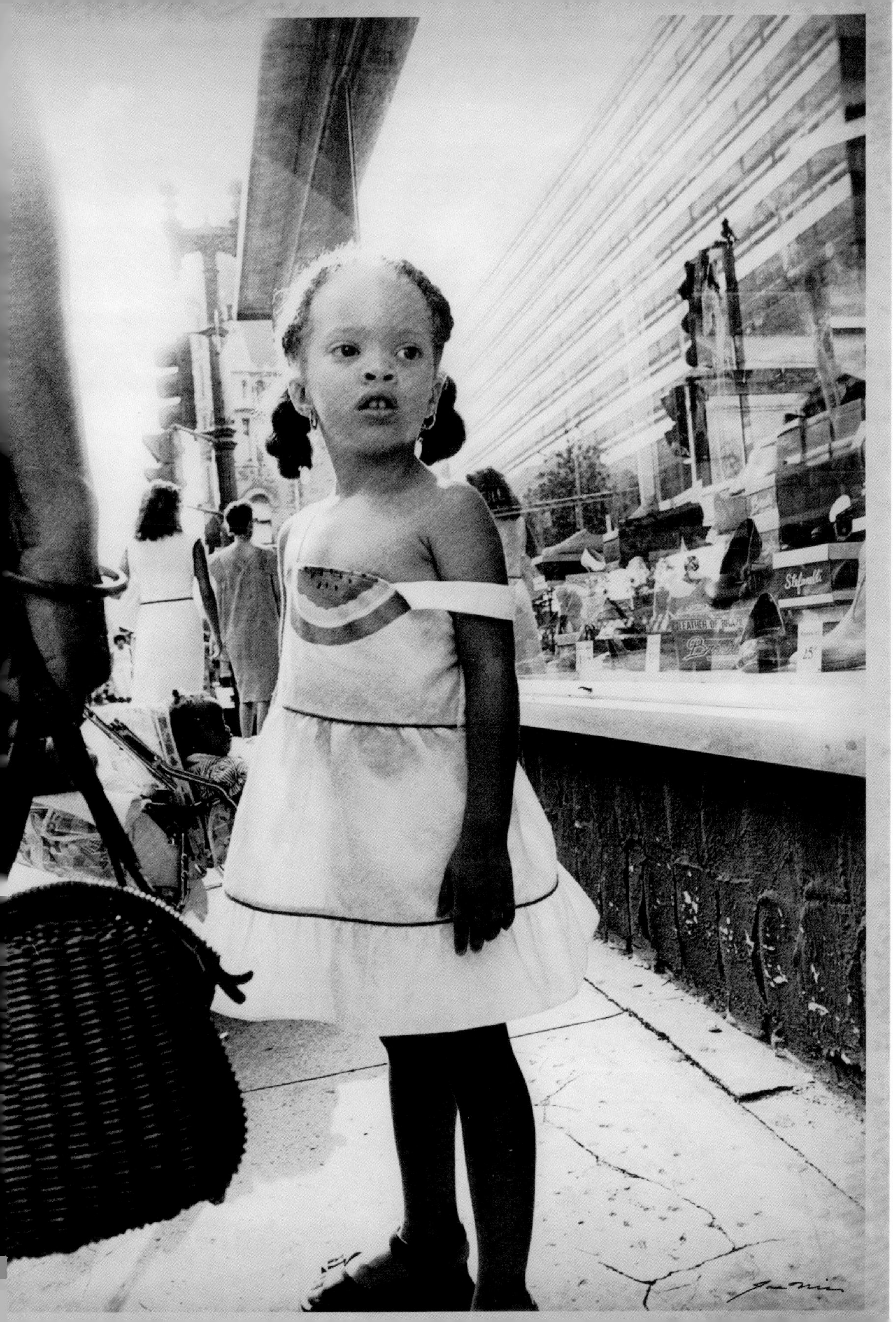

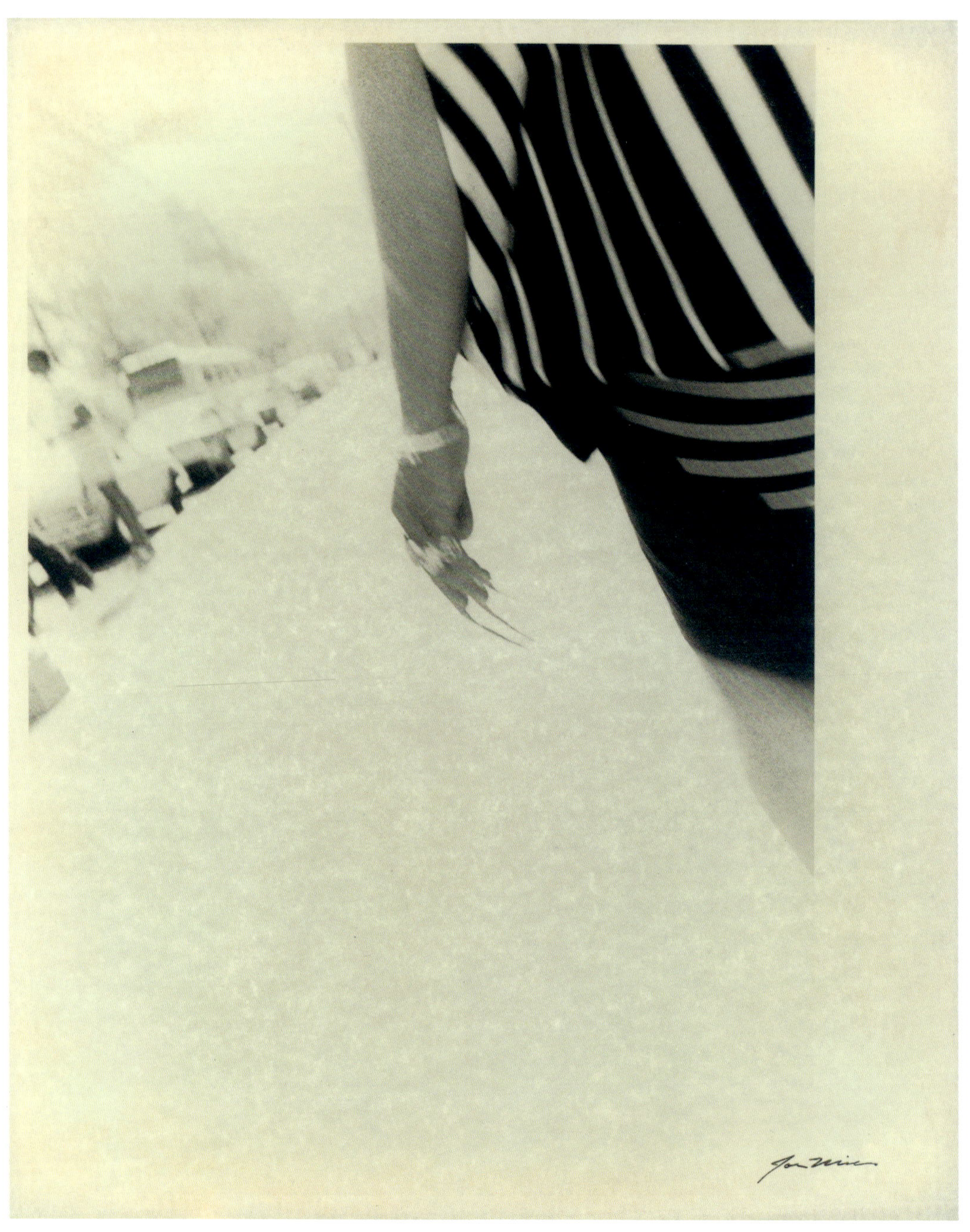

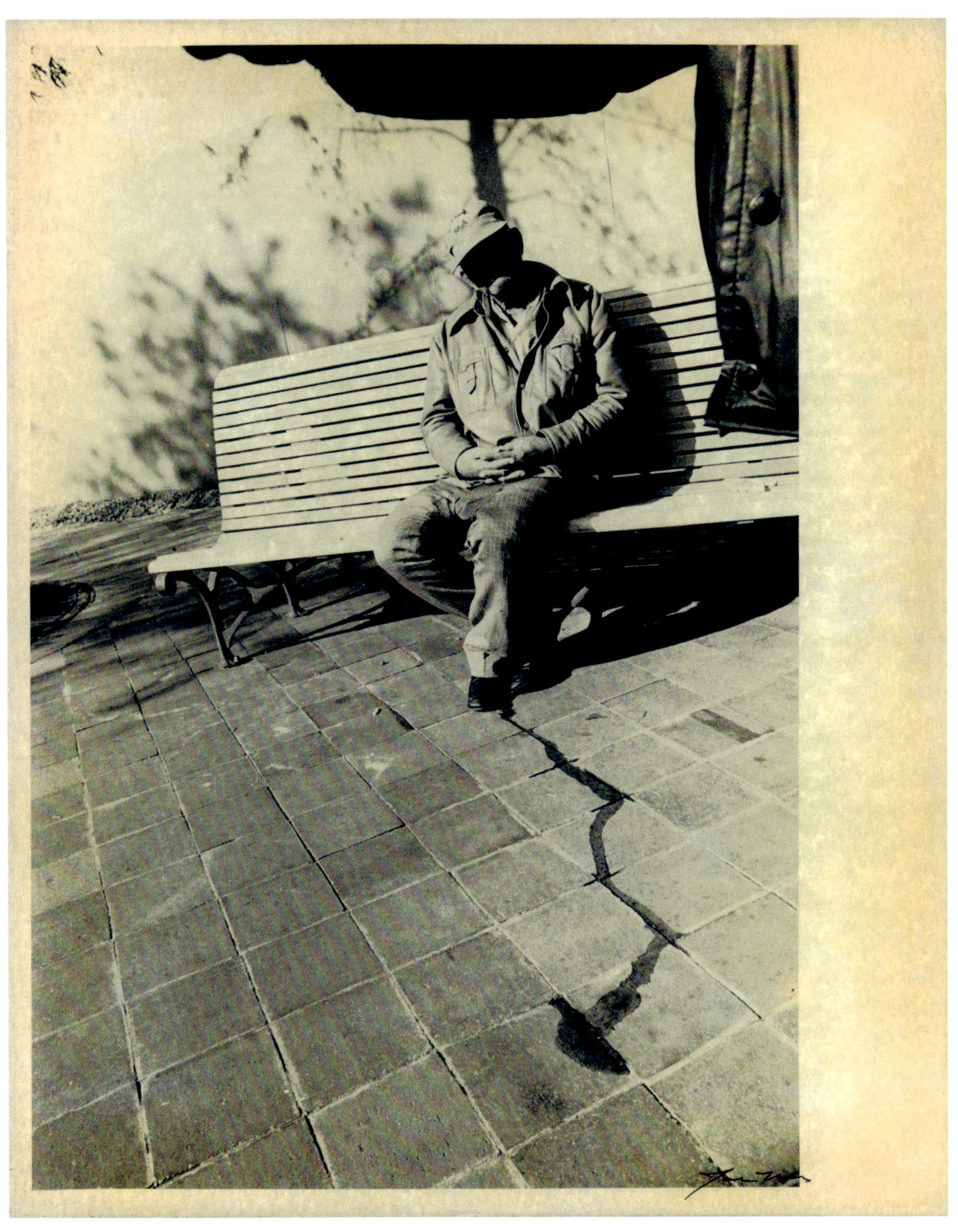

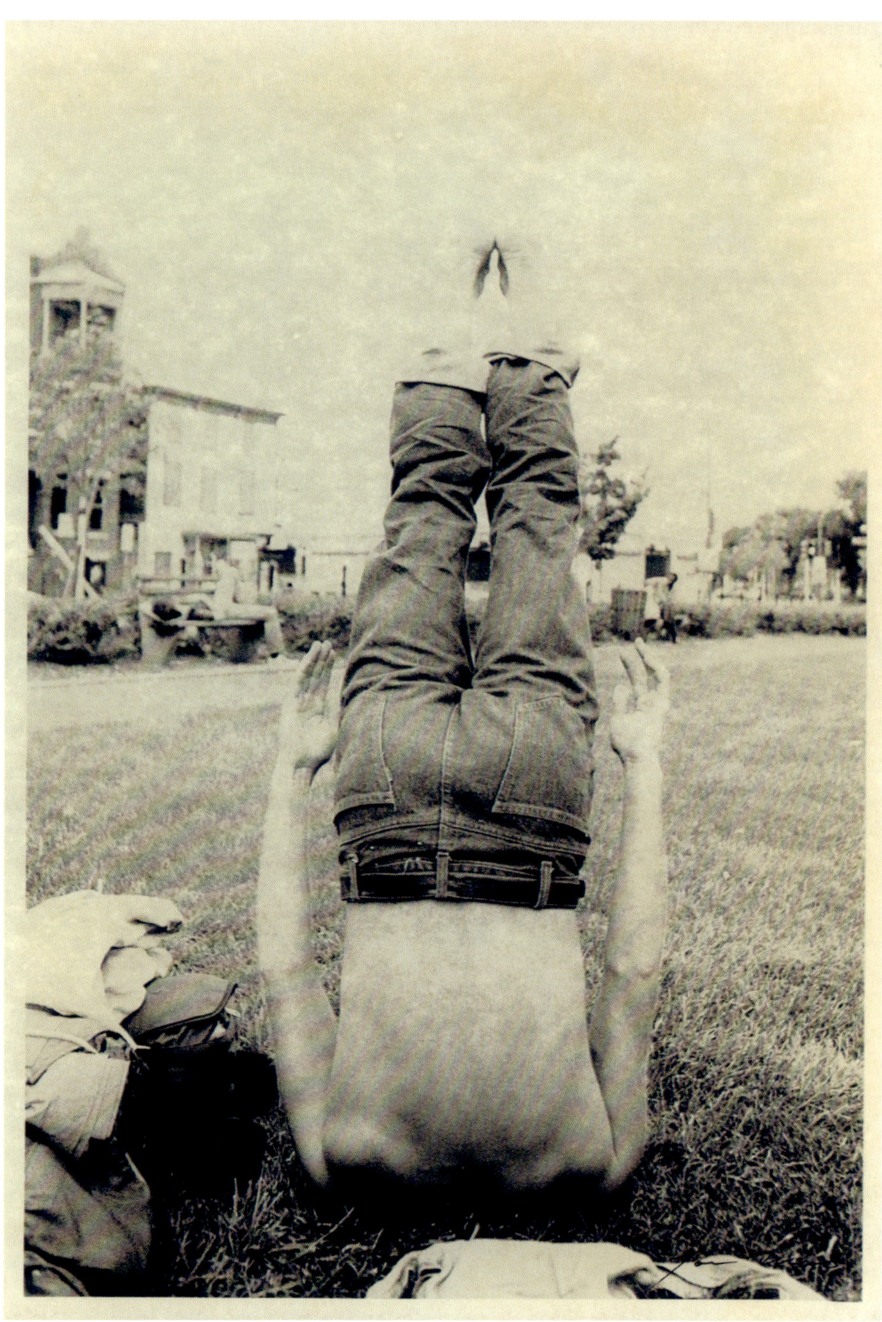

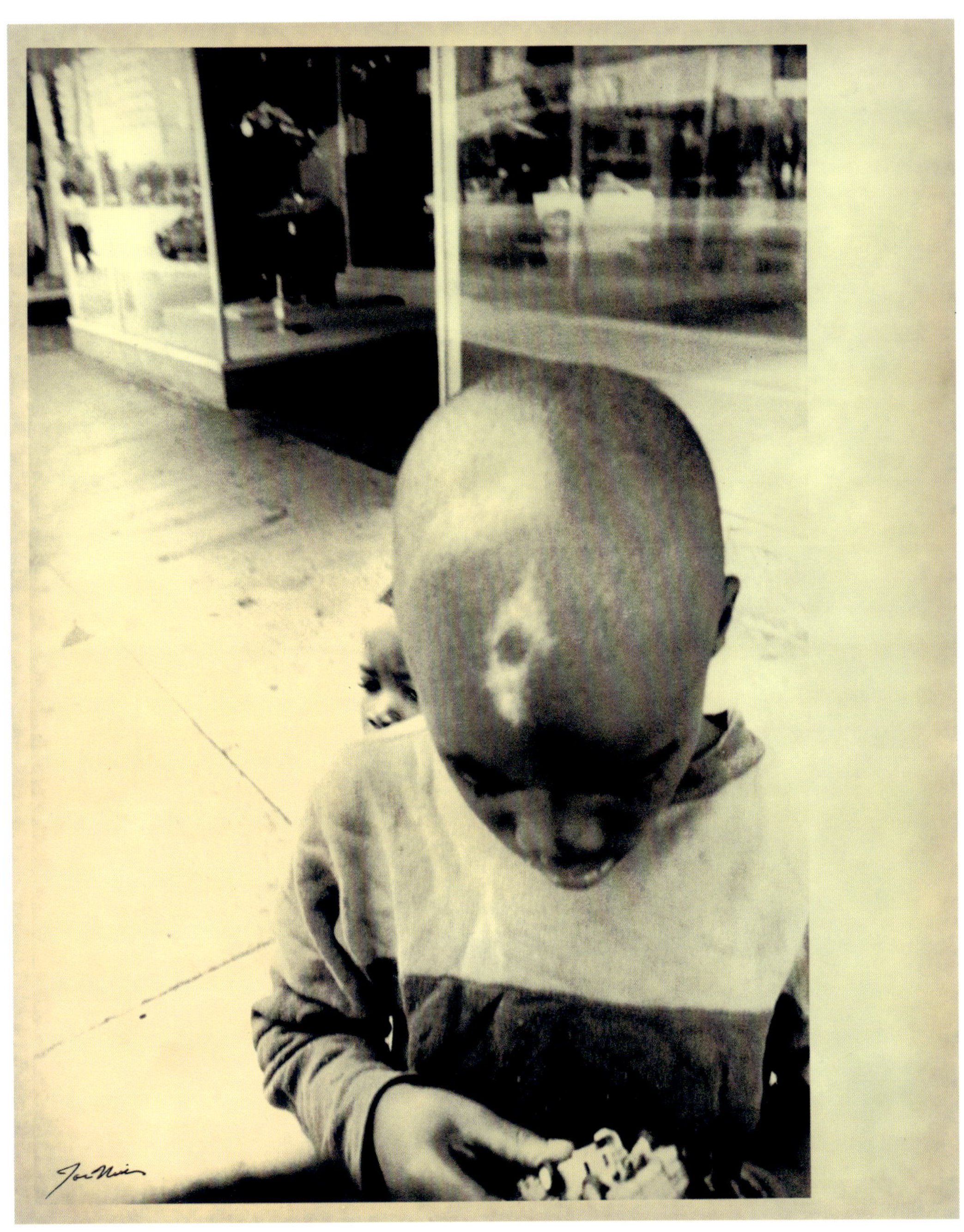

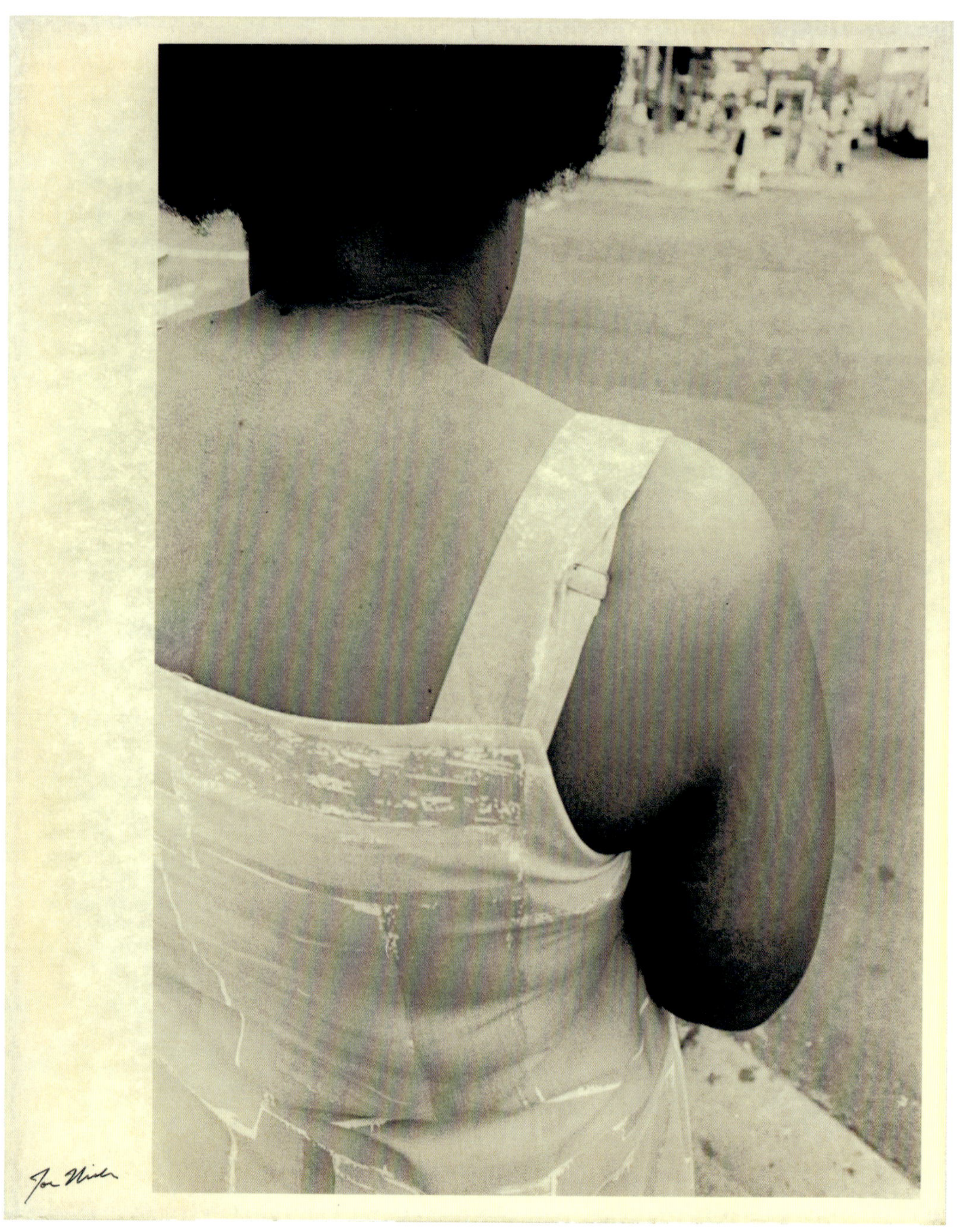

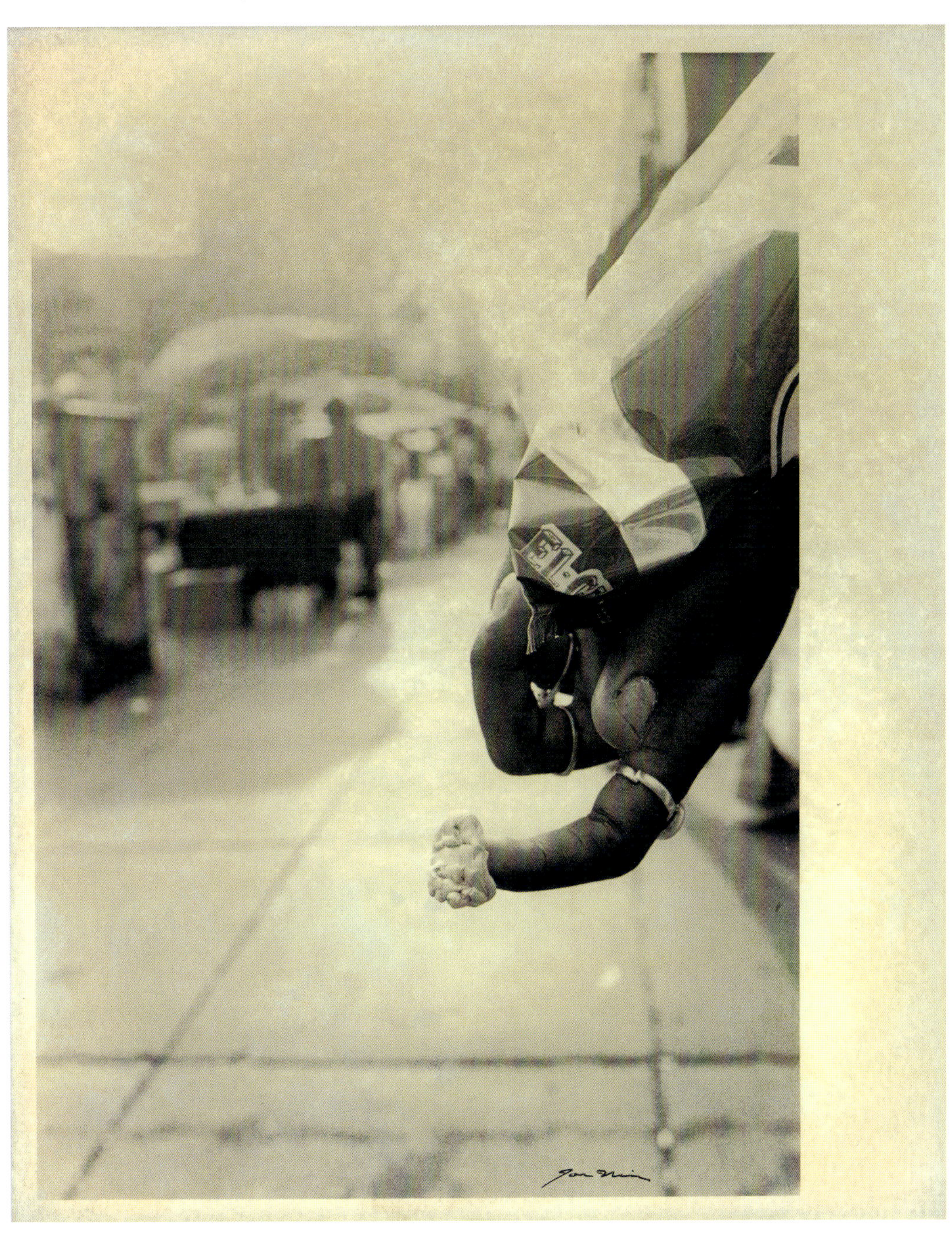

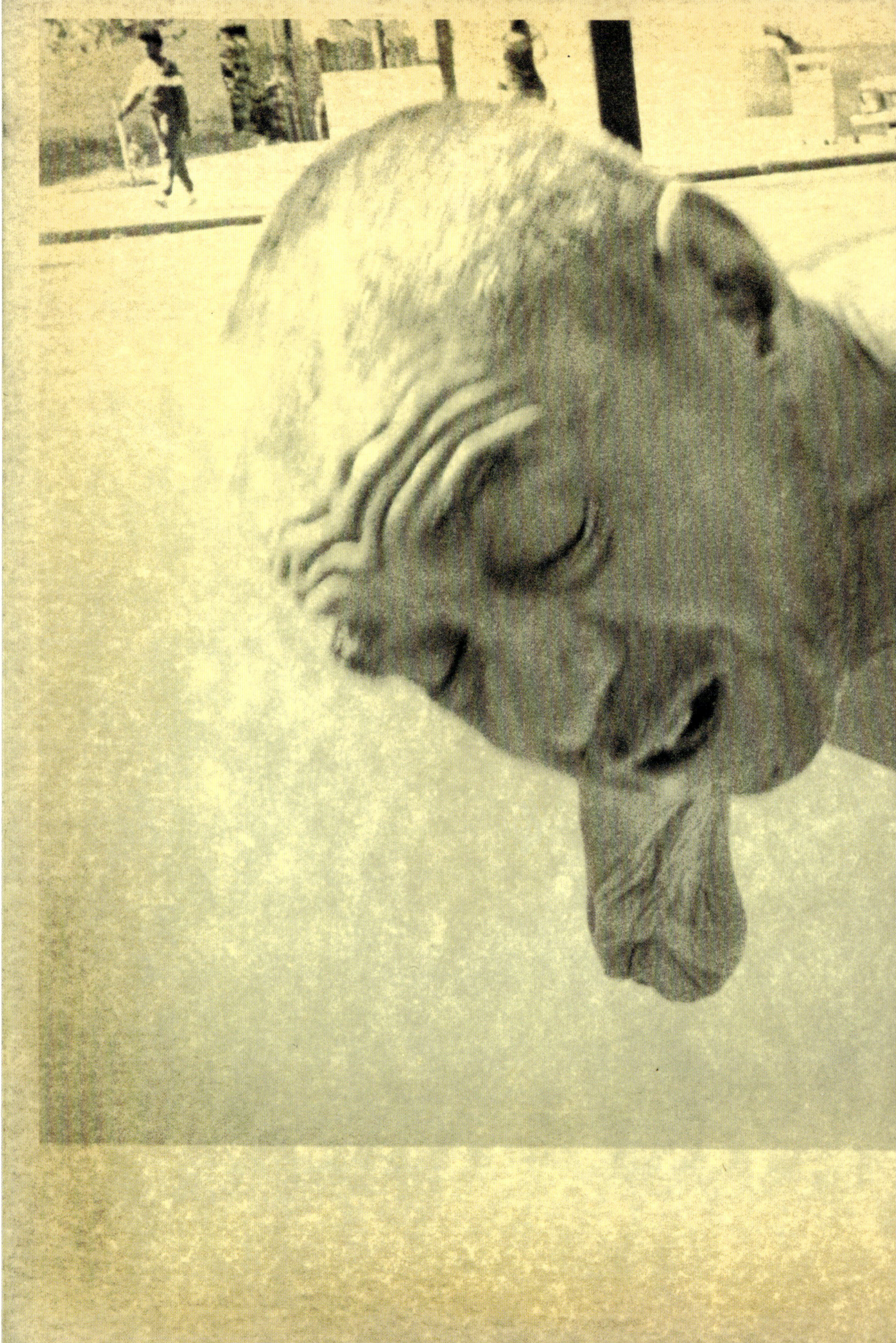

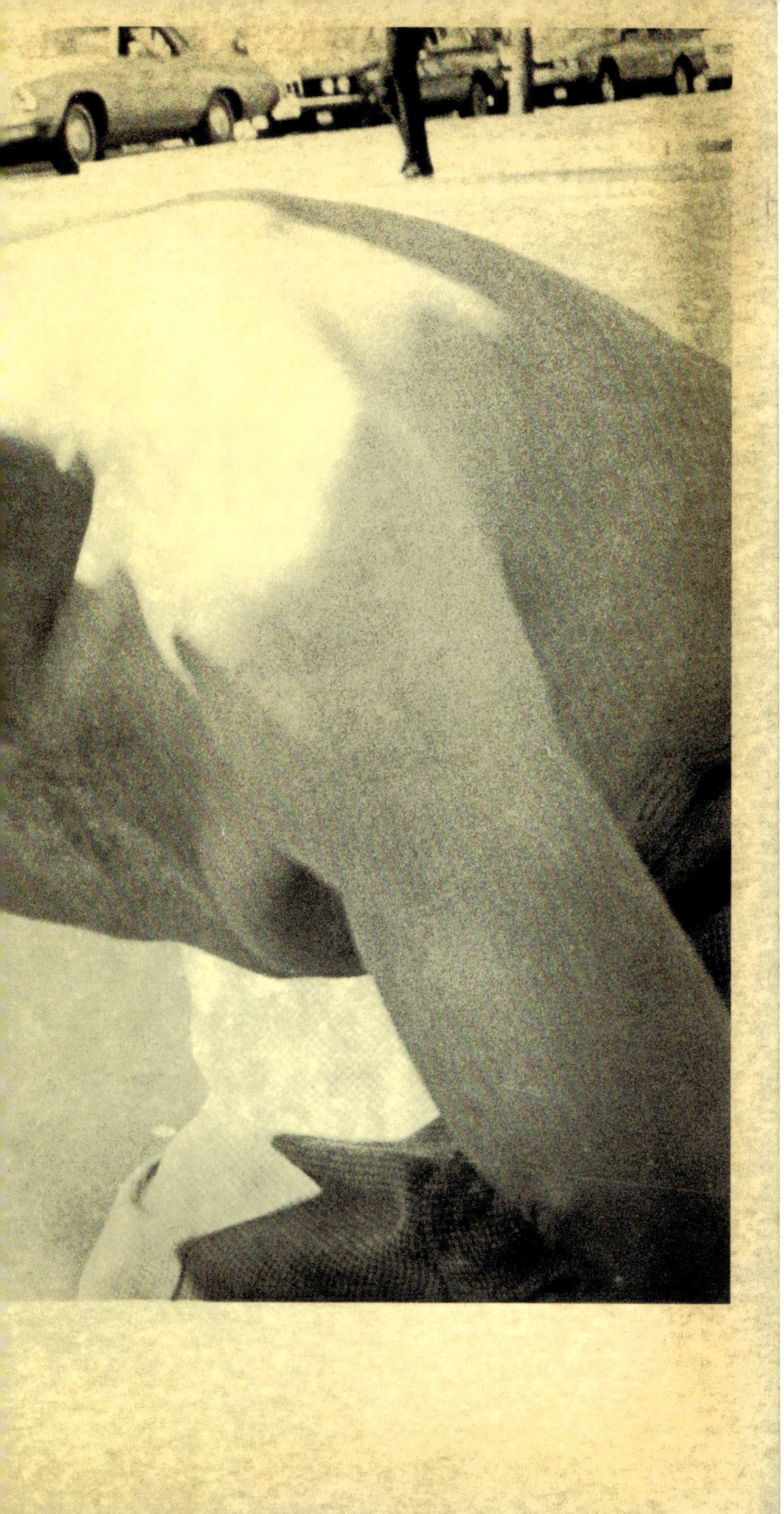

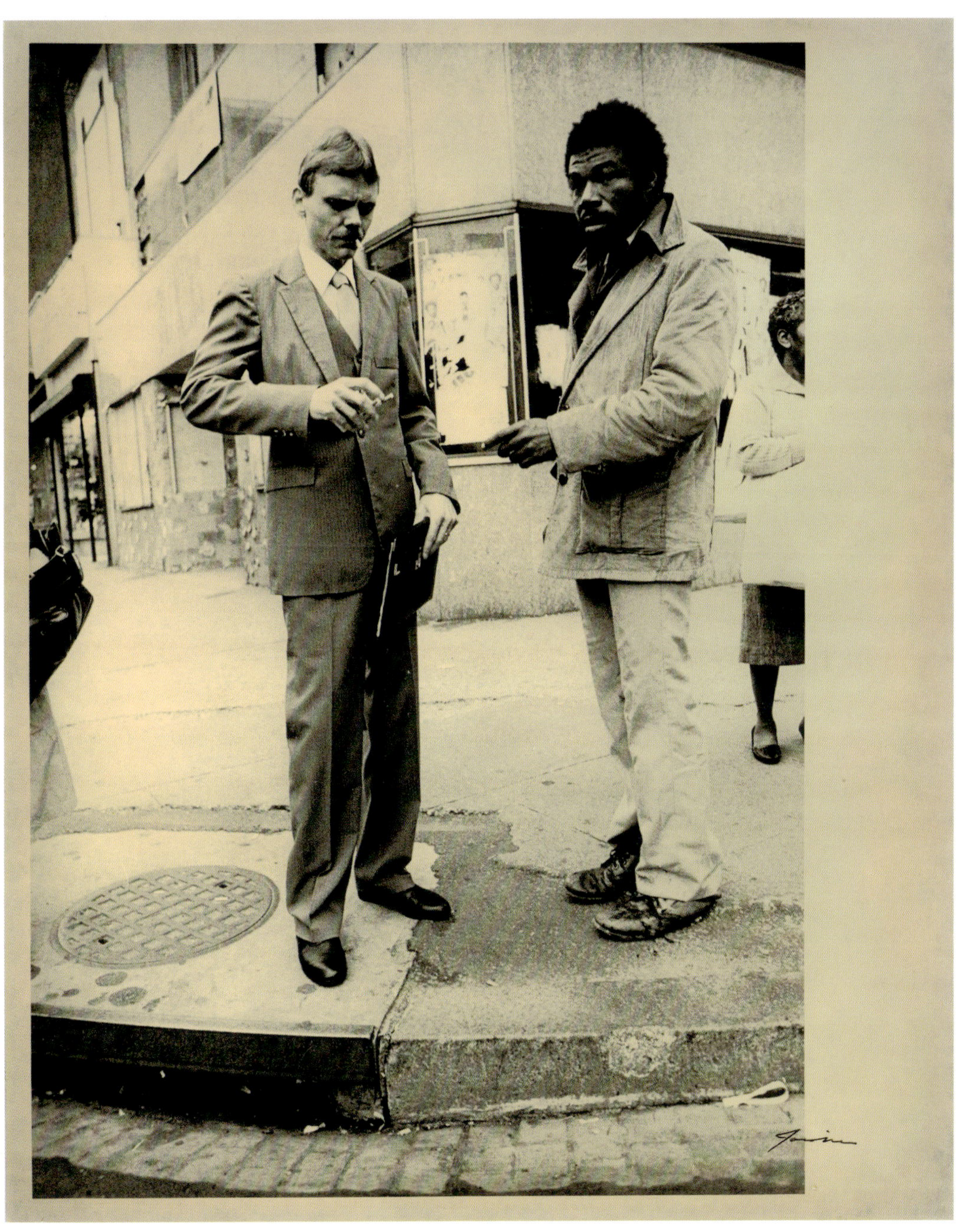

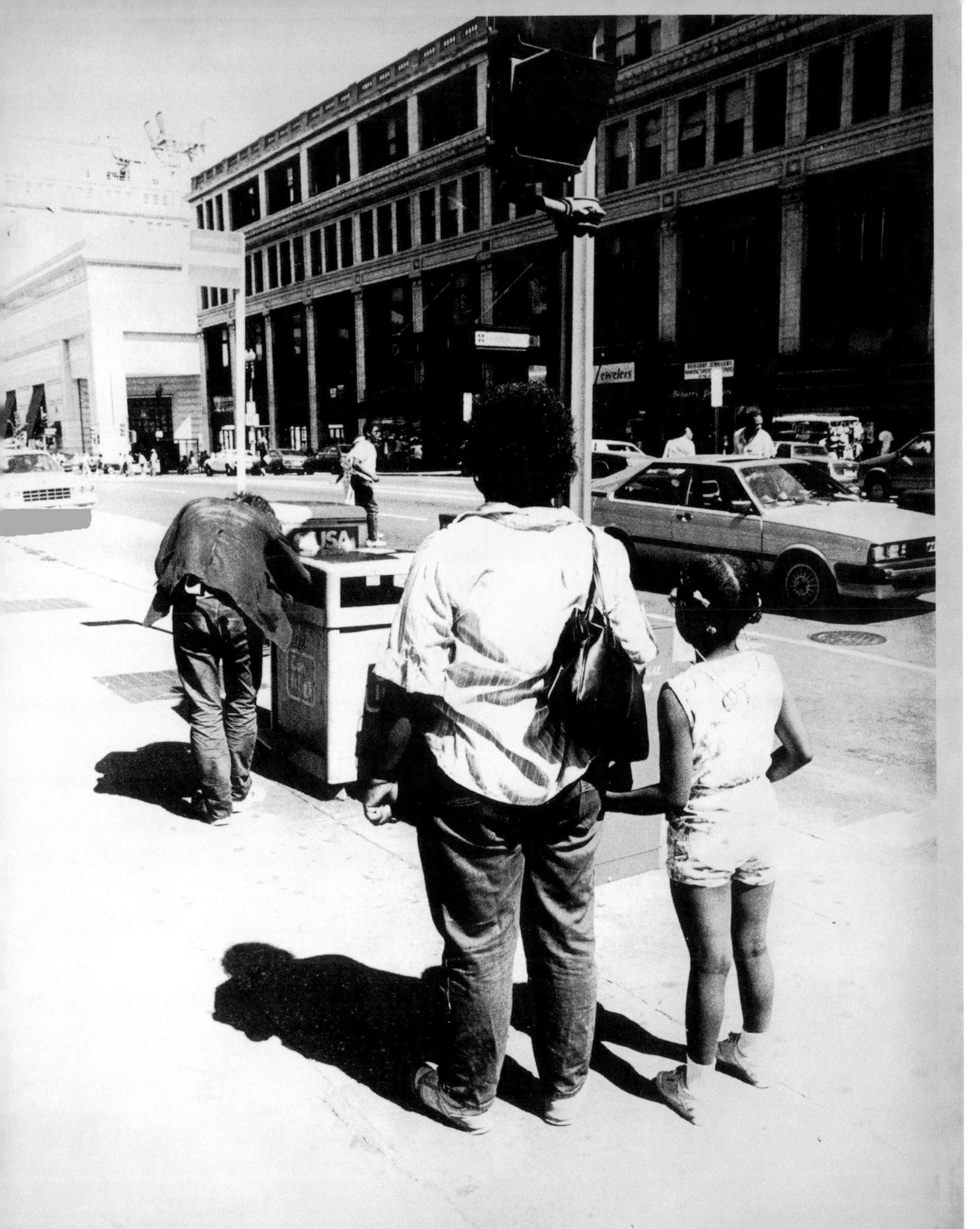

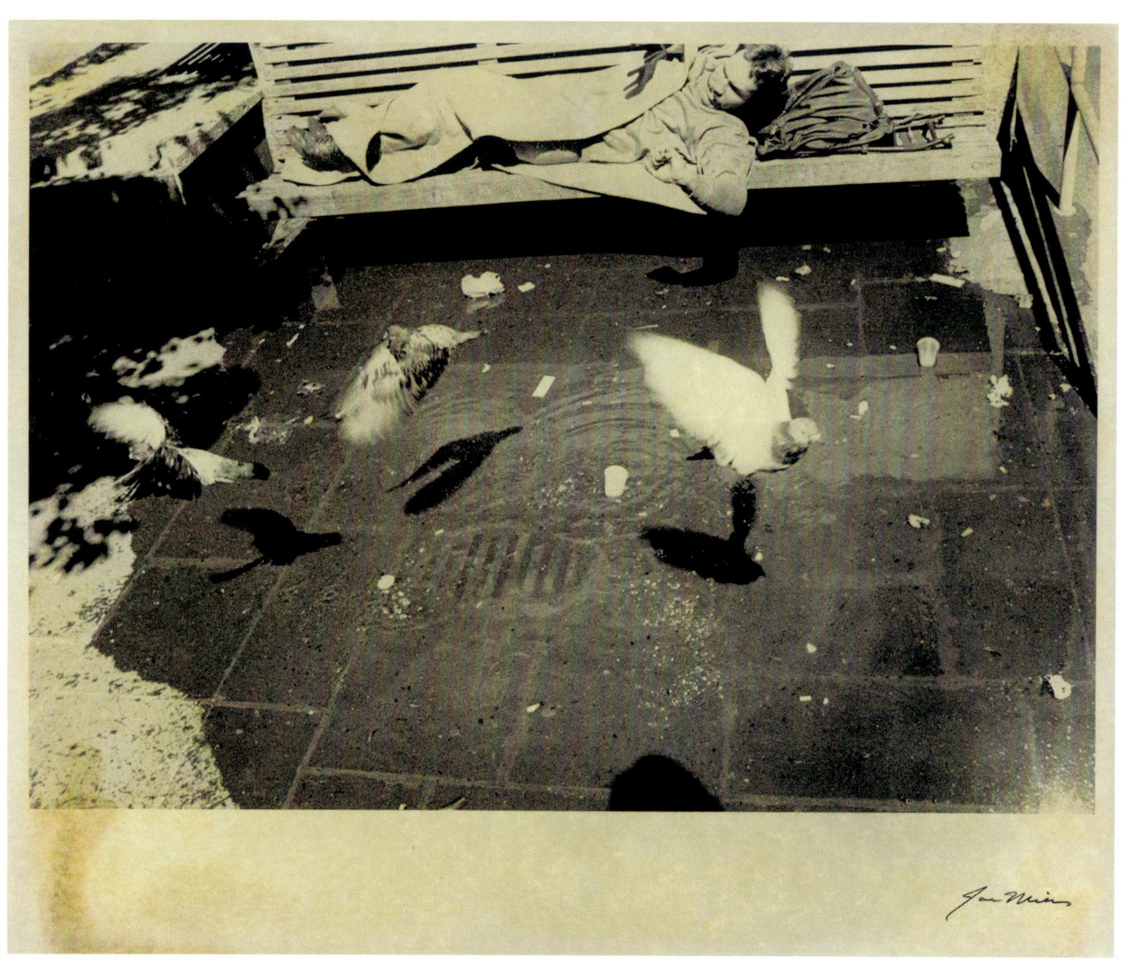

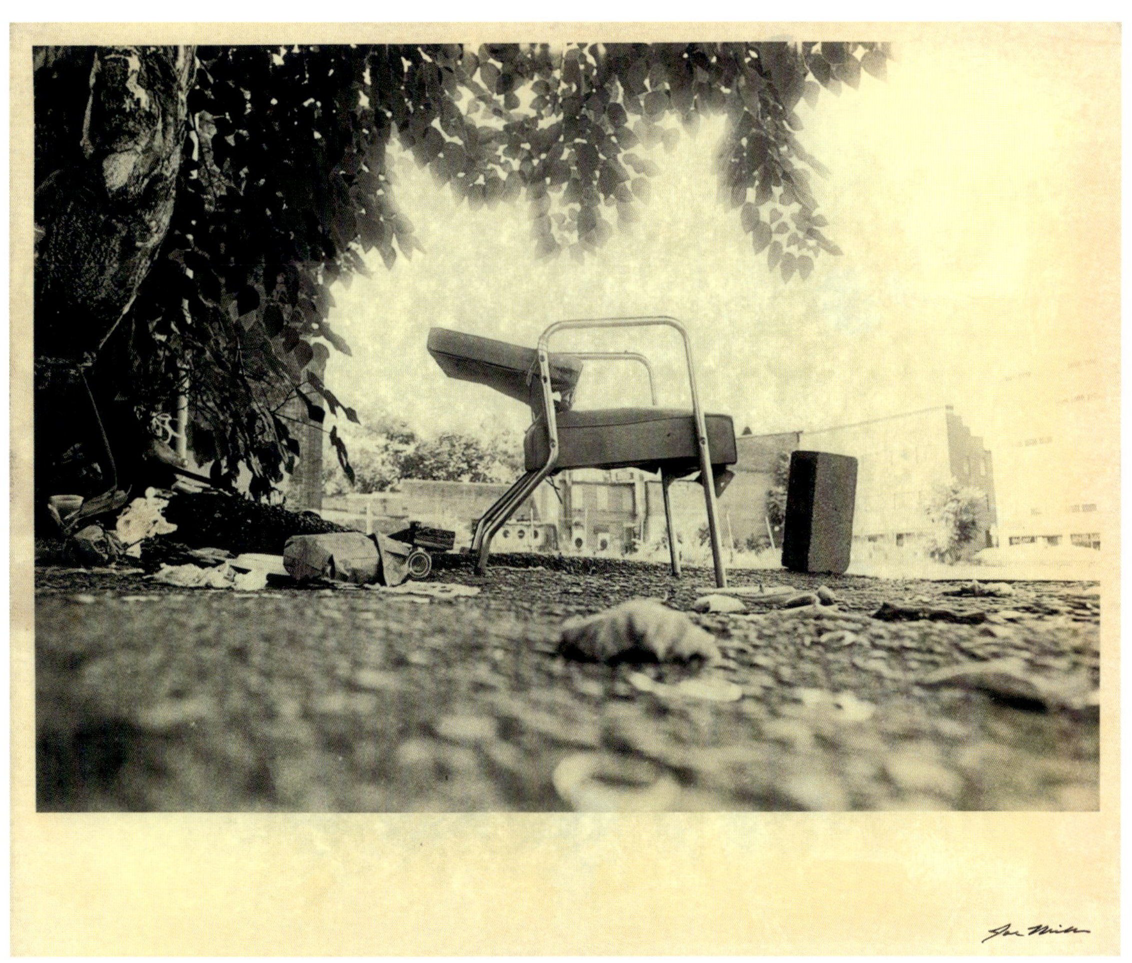

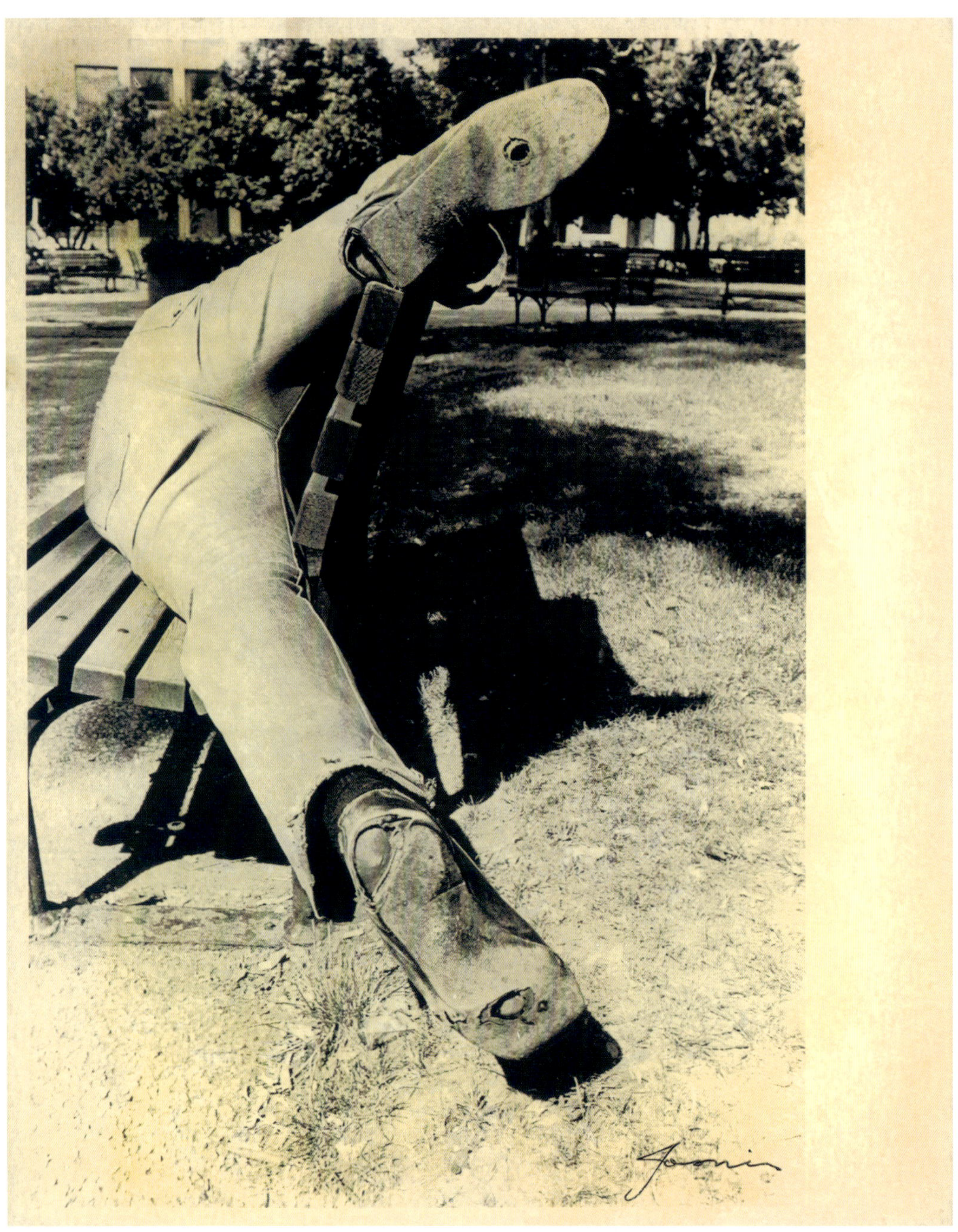

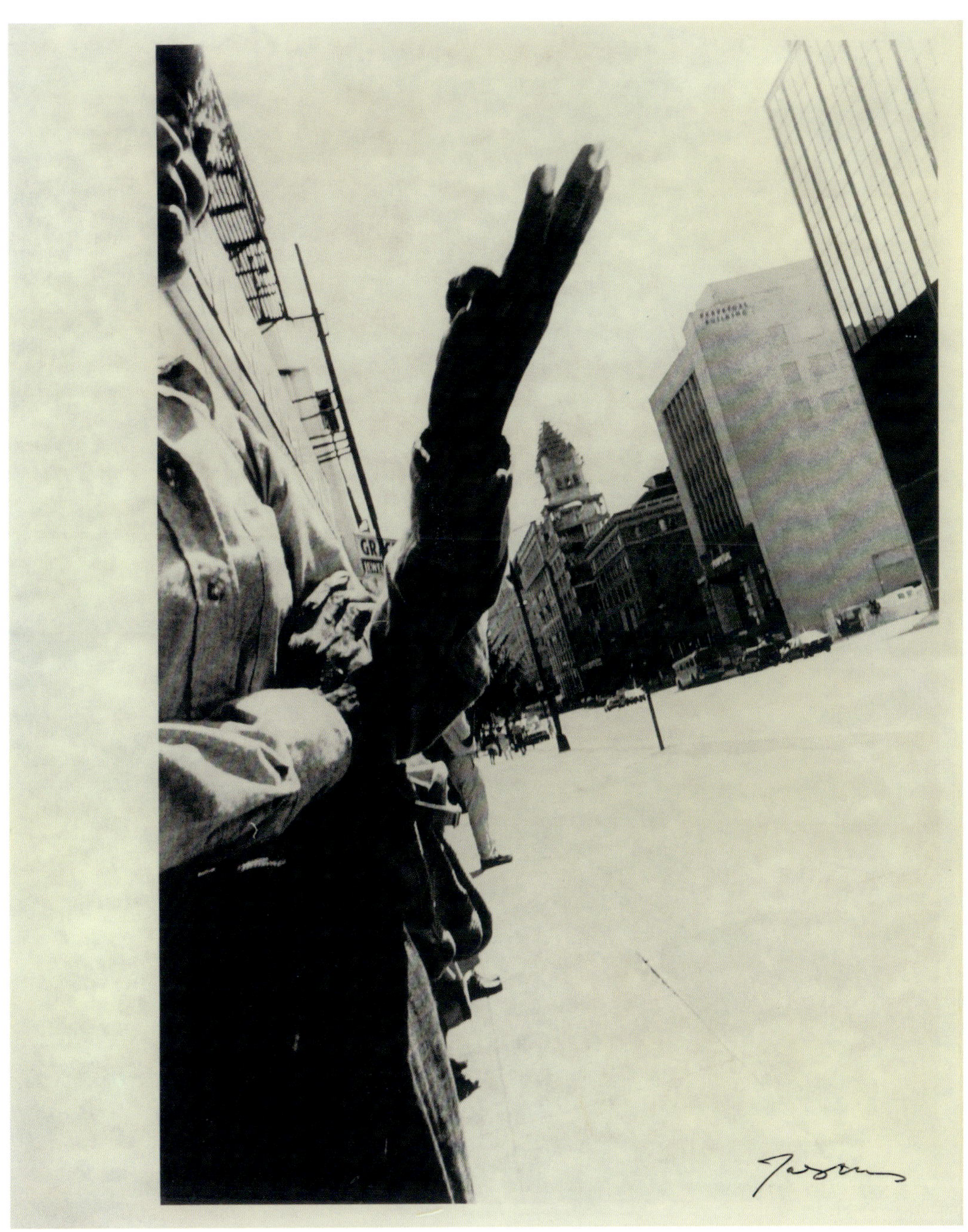

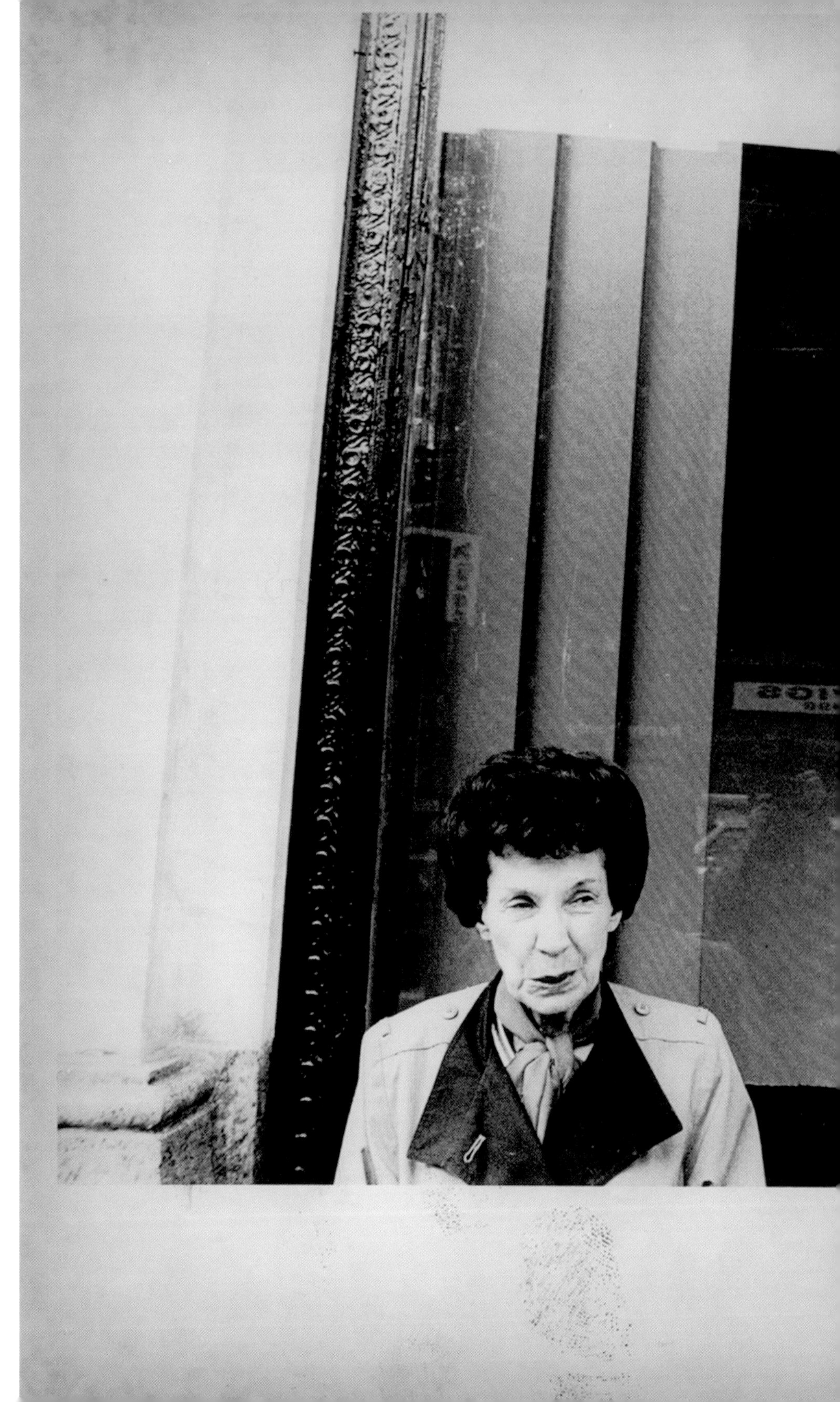

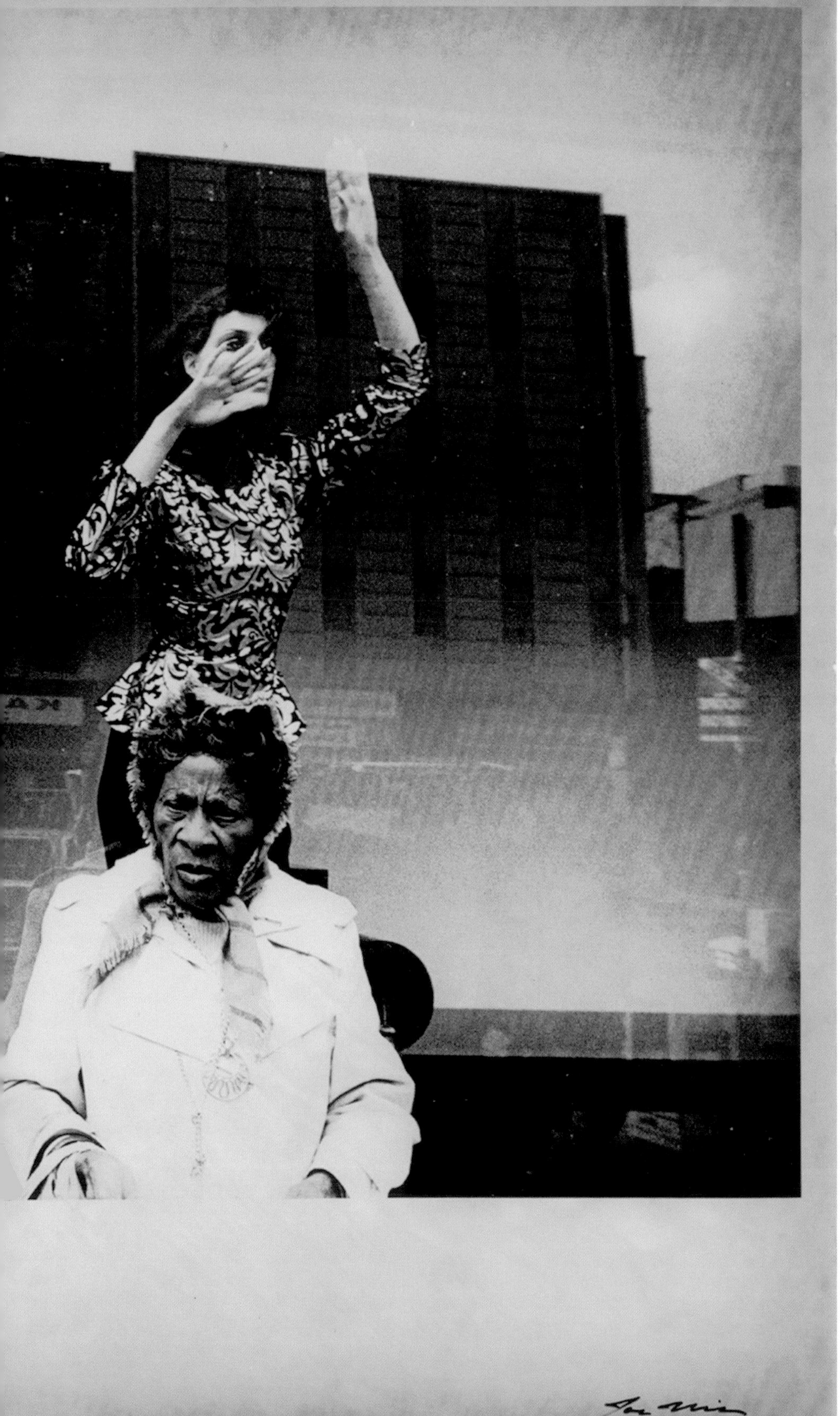

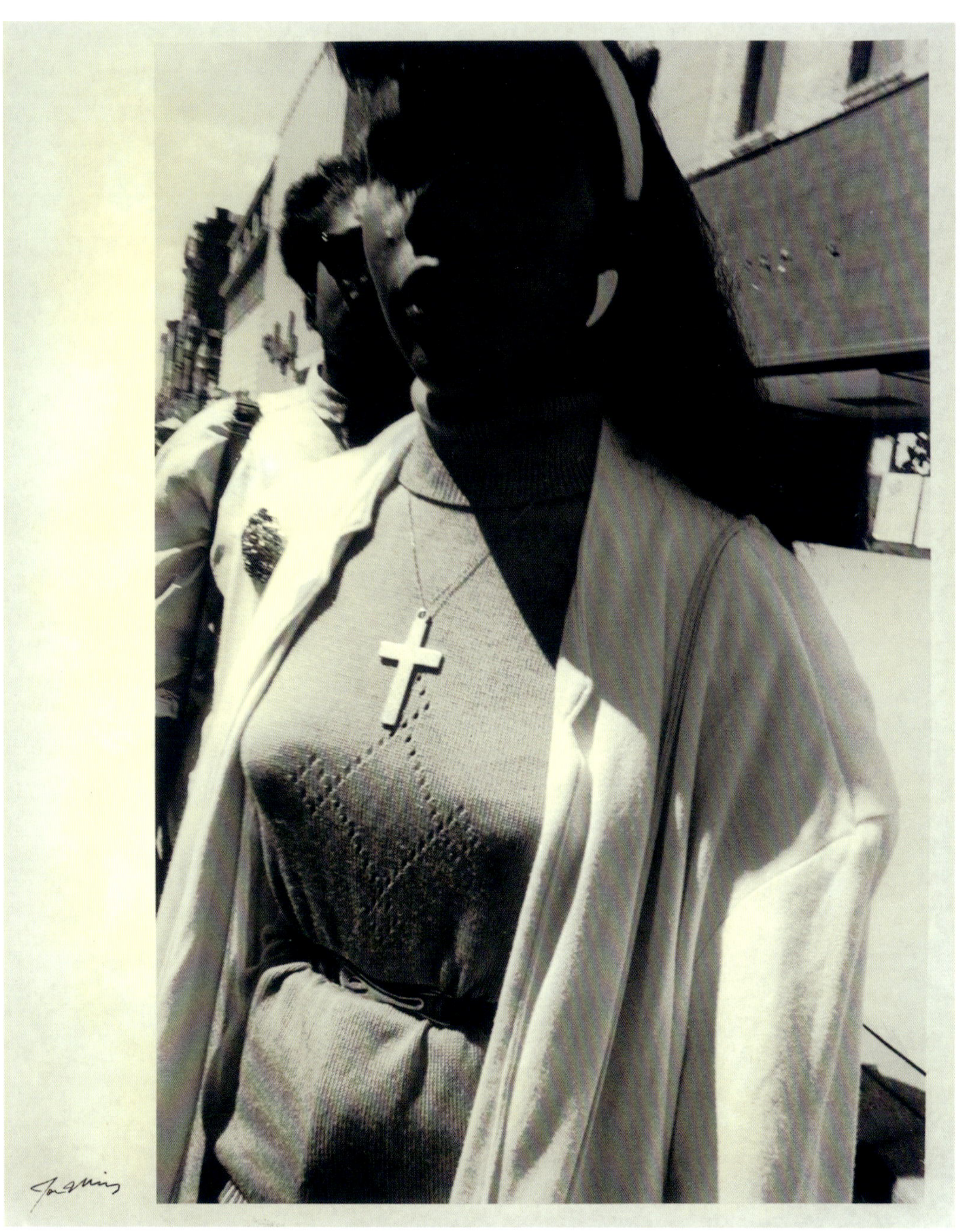

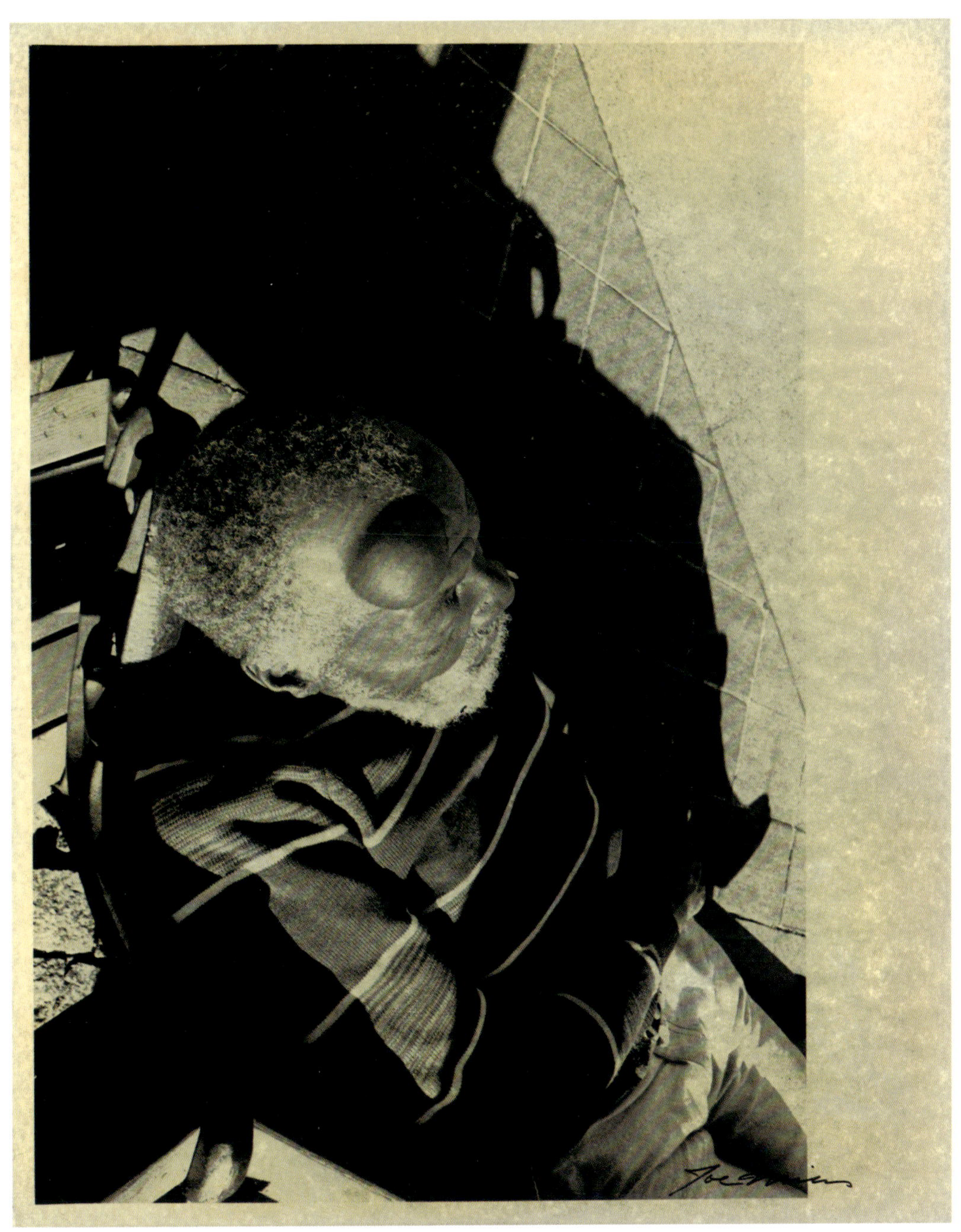

23

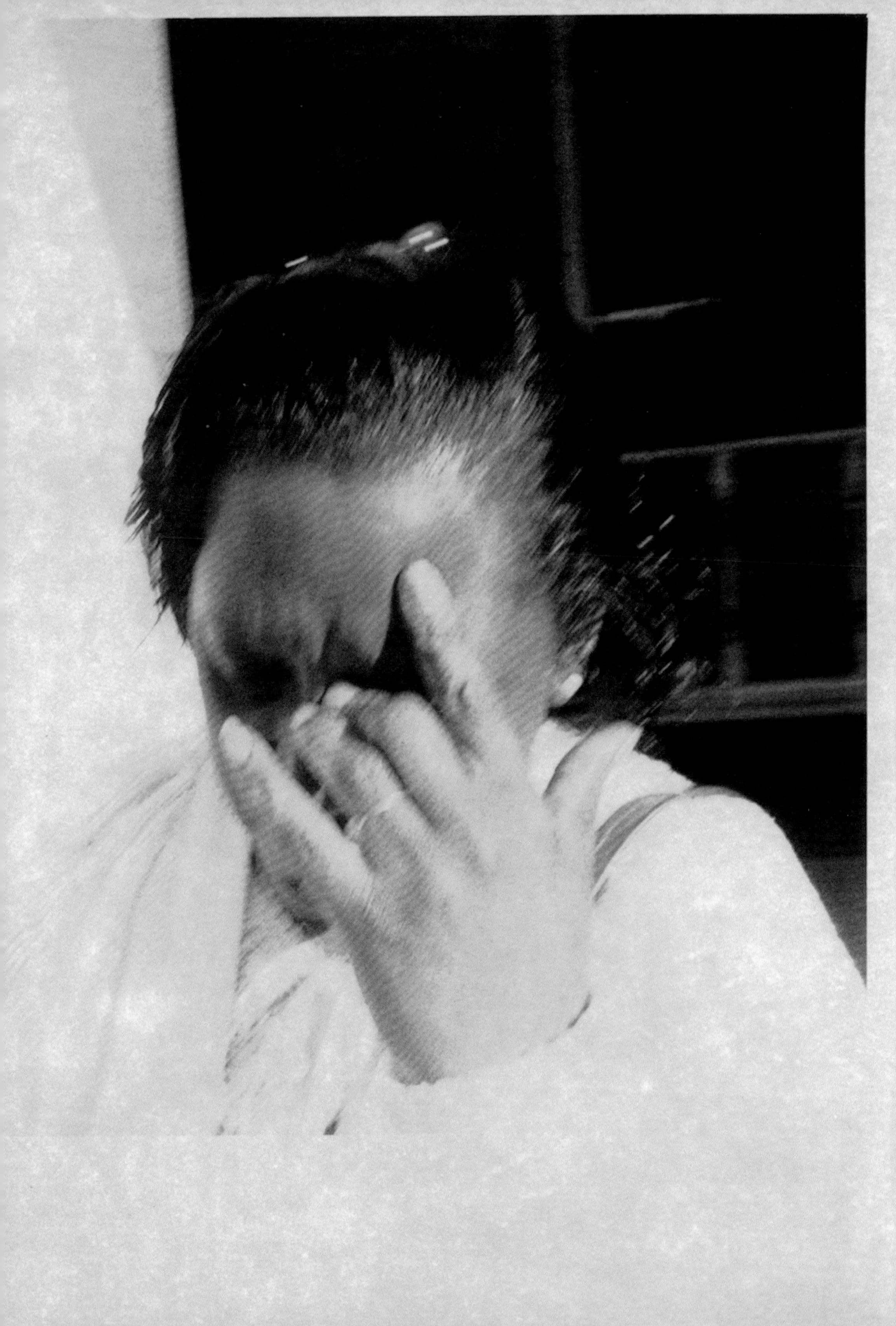

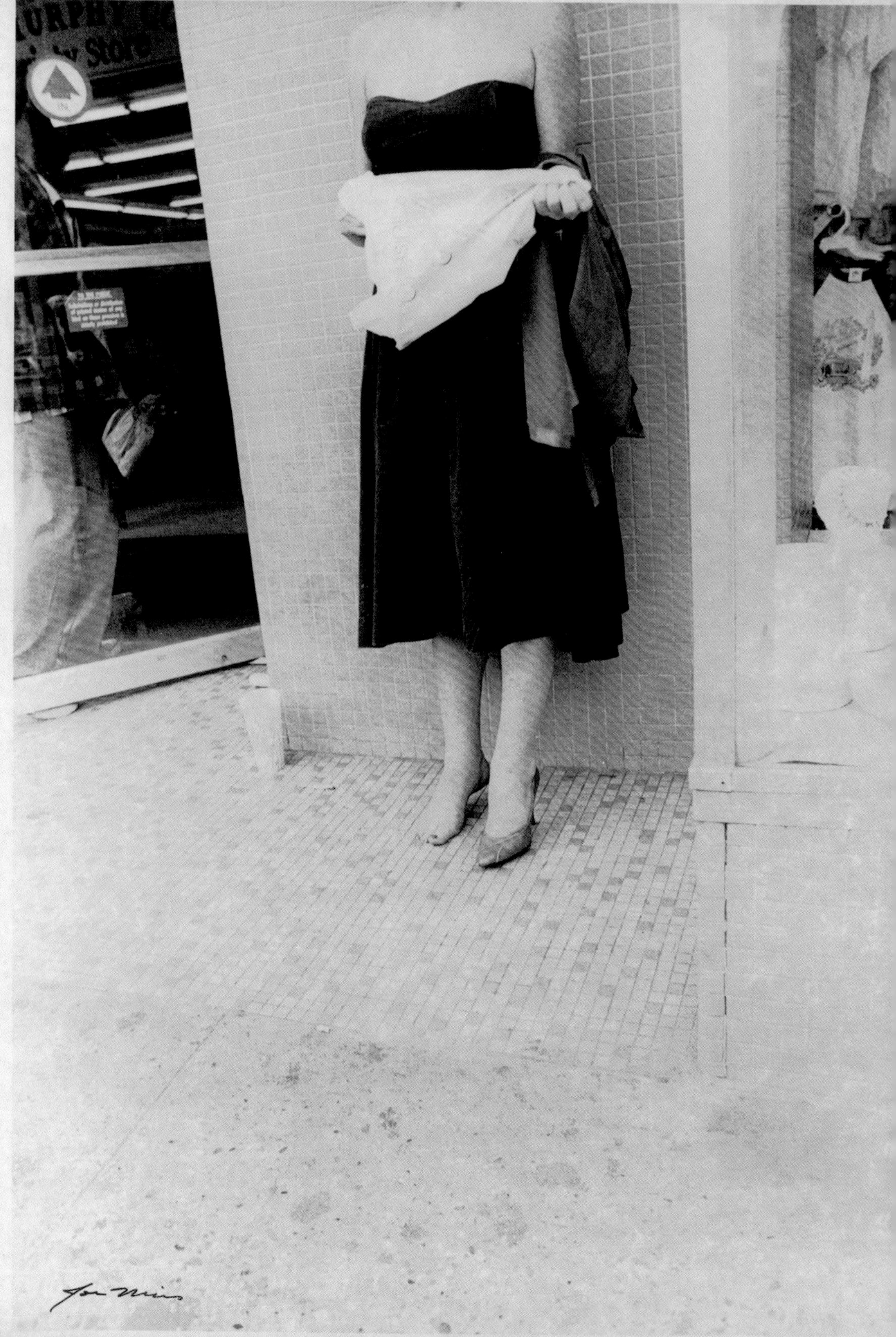
MURPHY
Store

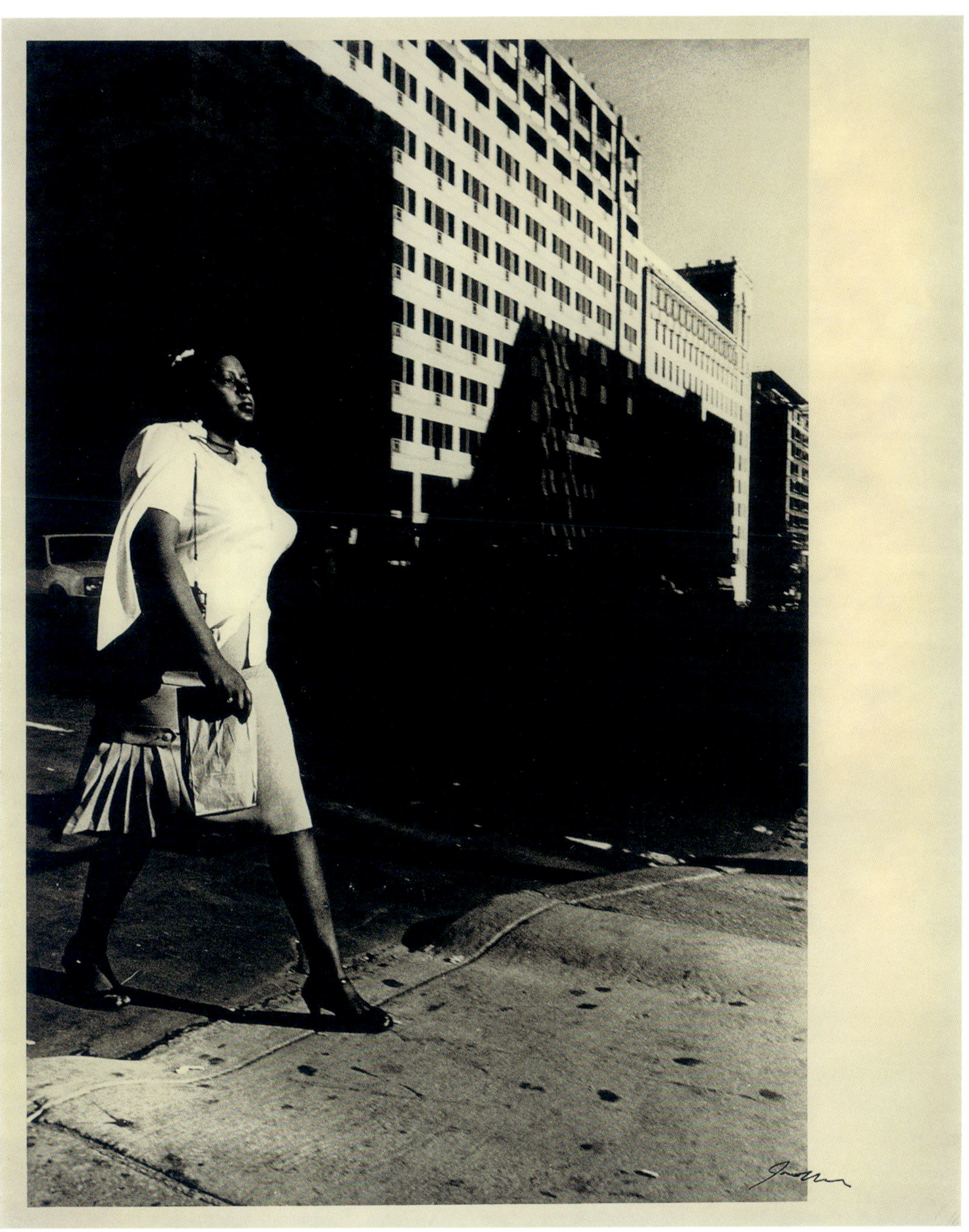

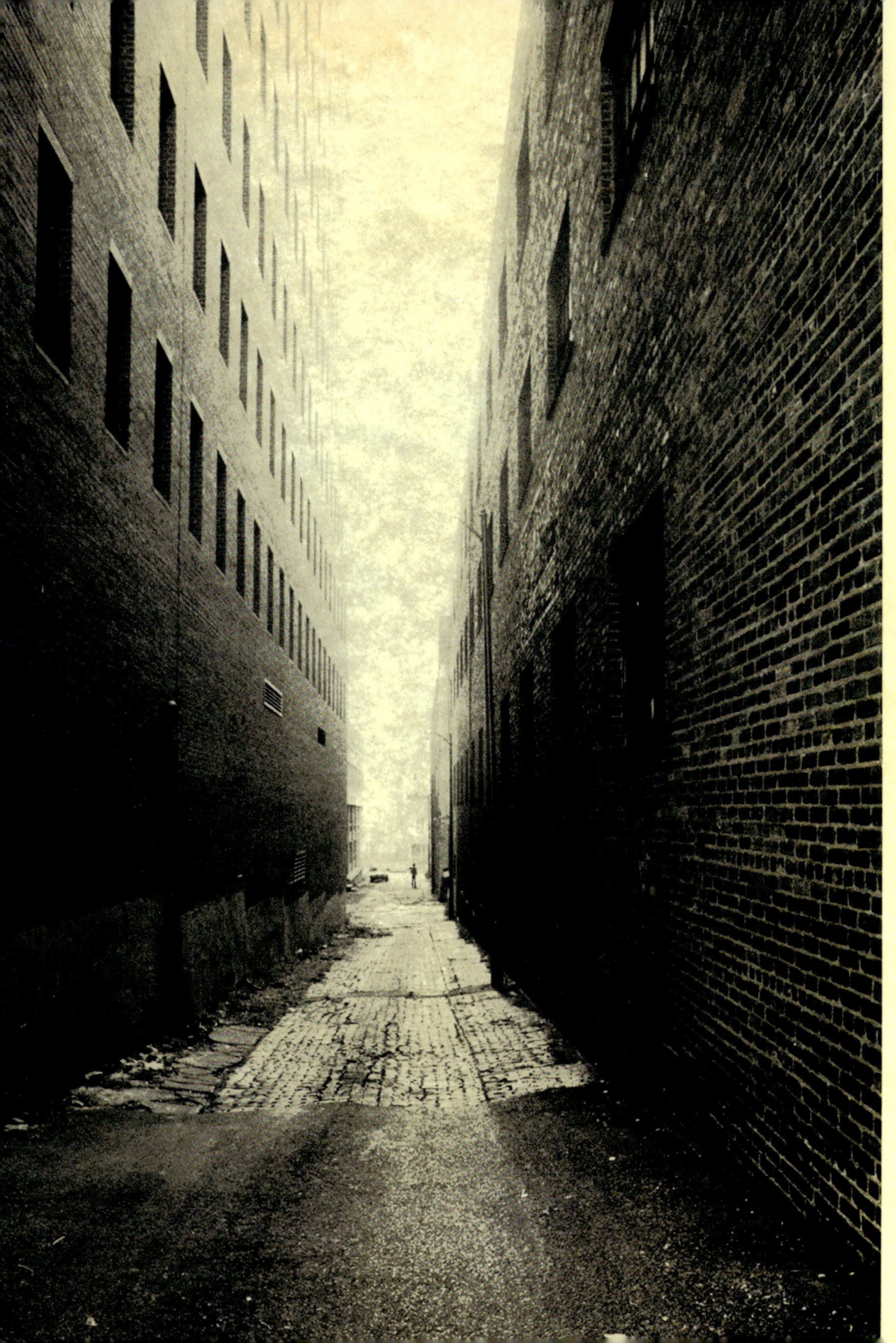

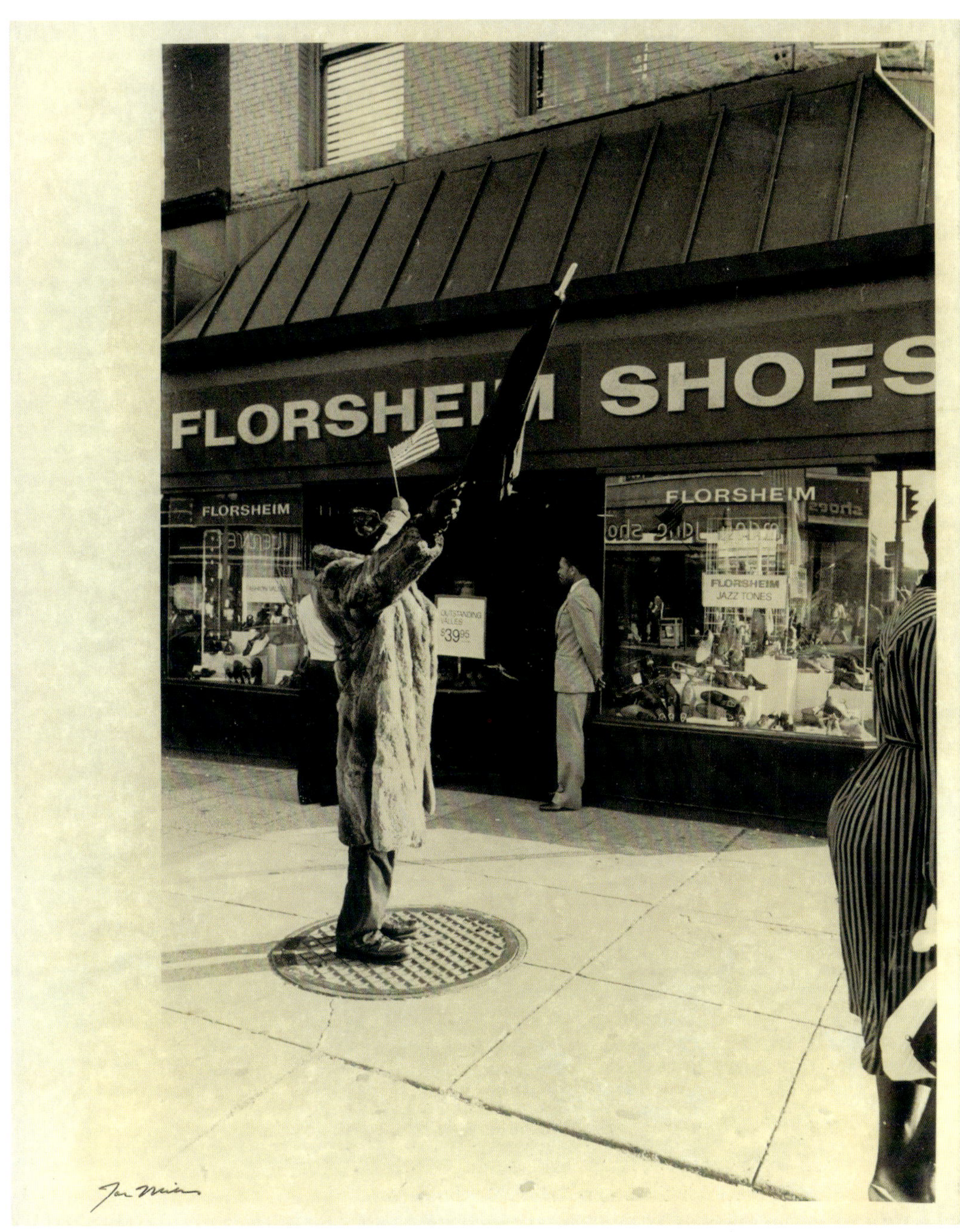

FLORSHEIM SHOES
FLORSHEIM
FLORSHEIM
JAZZ TONES
OUTSTANDING VALUES $39.95

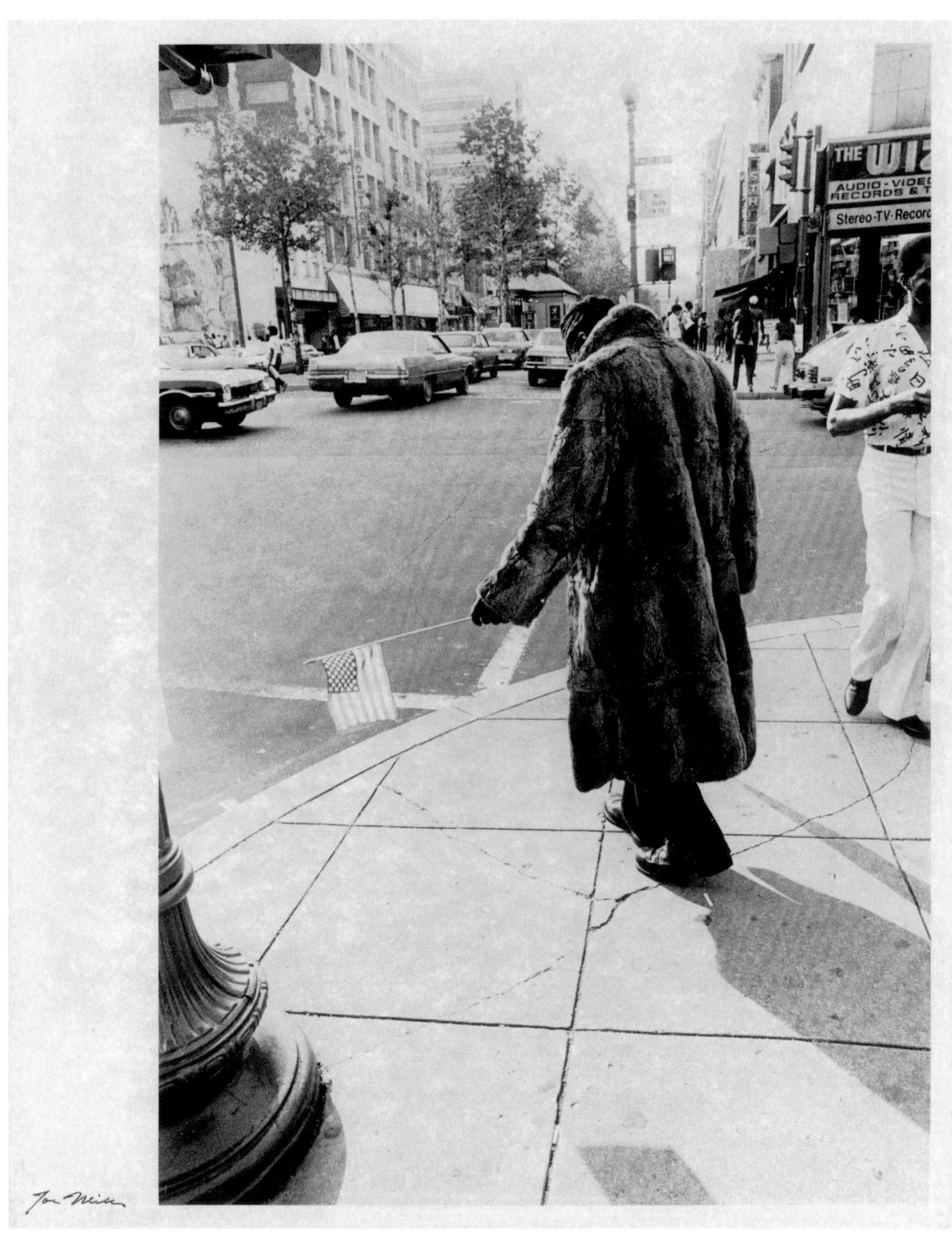

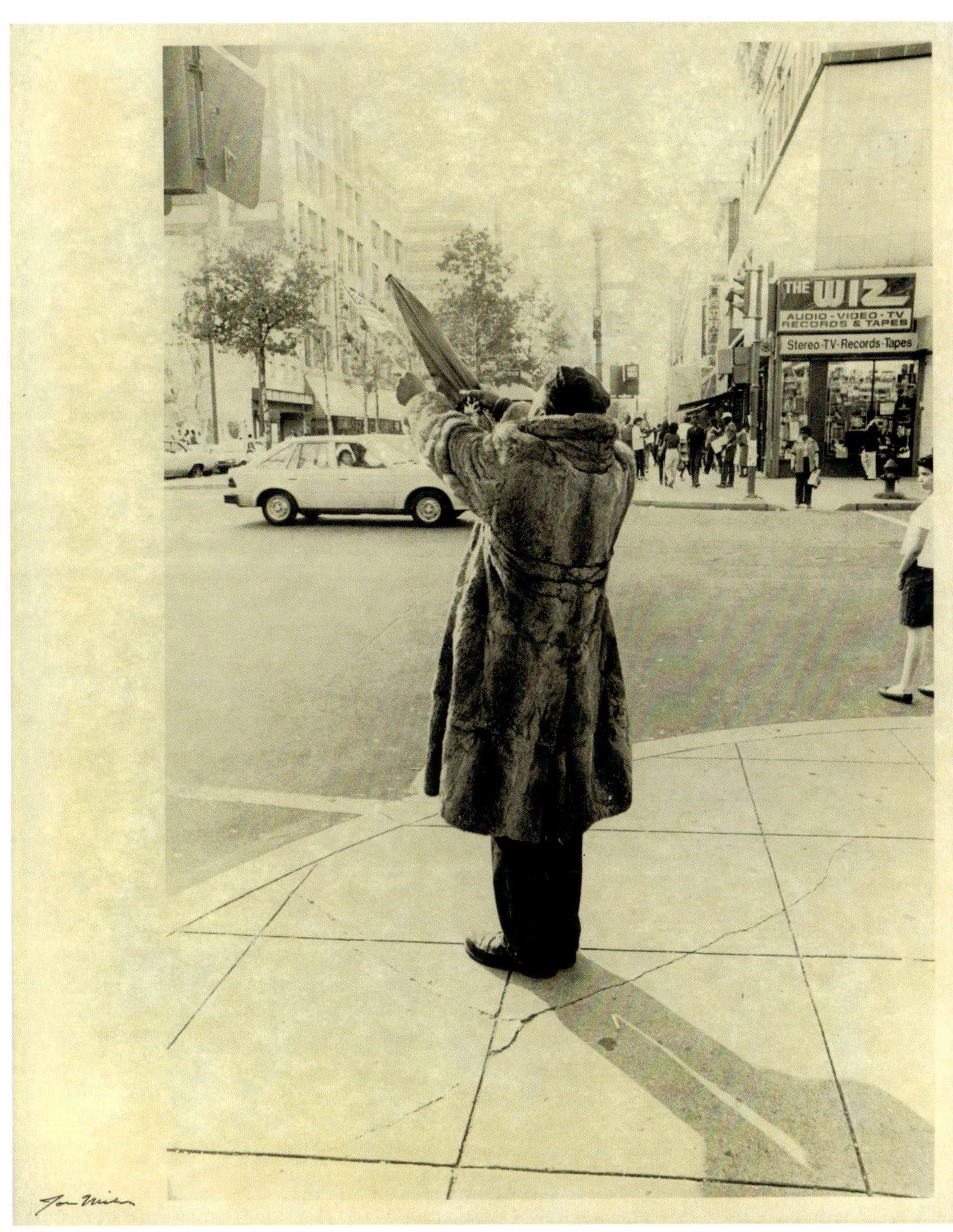
THE WIZ
AUDIO · VIDEO · TV
RECORDS & TAPES
Stereo · TV · Records · Tapes

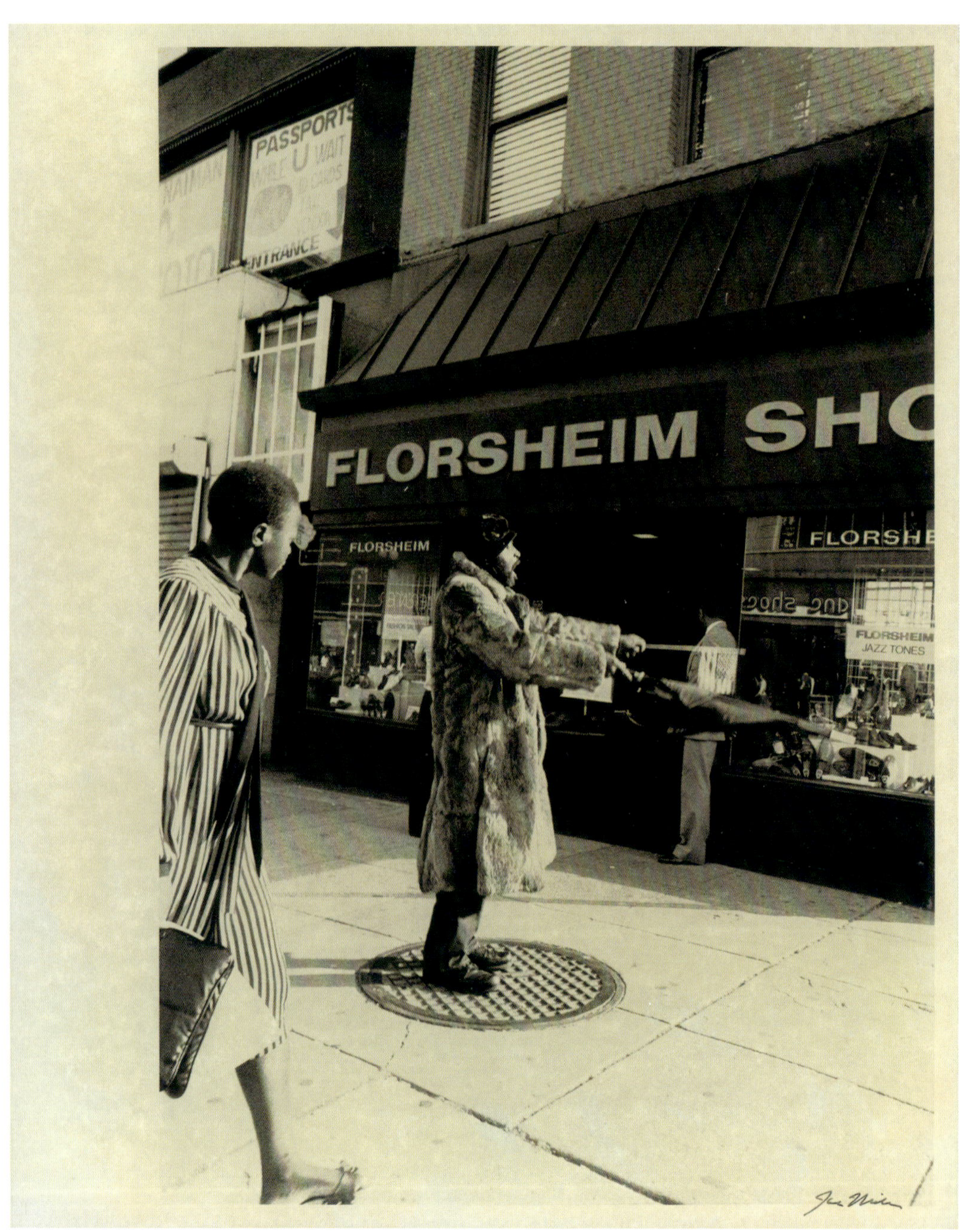

PASSPORTS
WHILE U WAIT
ENTRANCE
FLORSHEIM SHO
FLORSHEIM
FLORSHEIM
JAZZ TONES

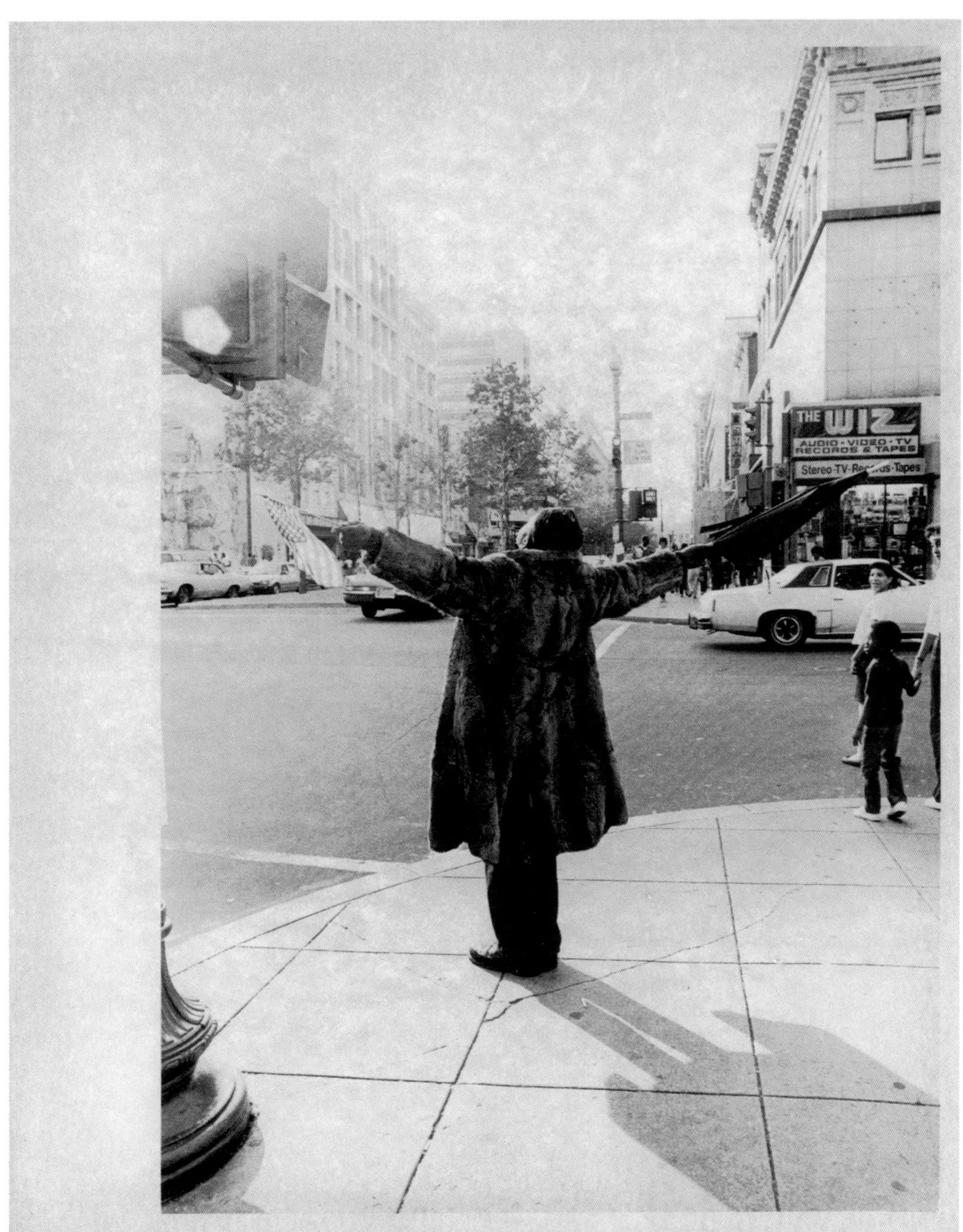

THE WIZ
AUDIO · VIDEO · TV
RECORDS & TAPES
Stereo · TV · Records · Tapes

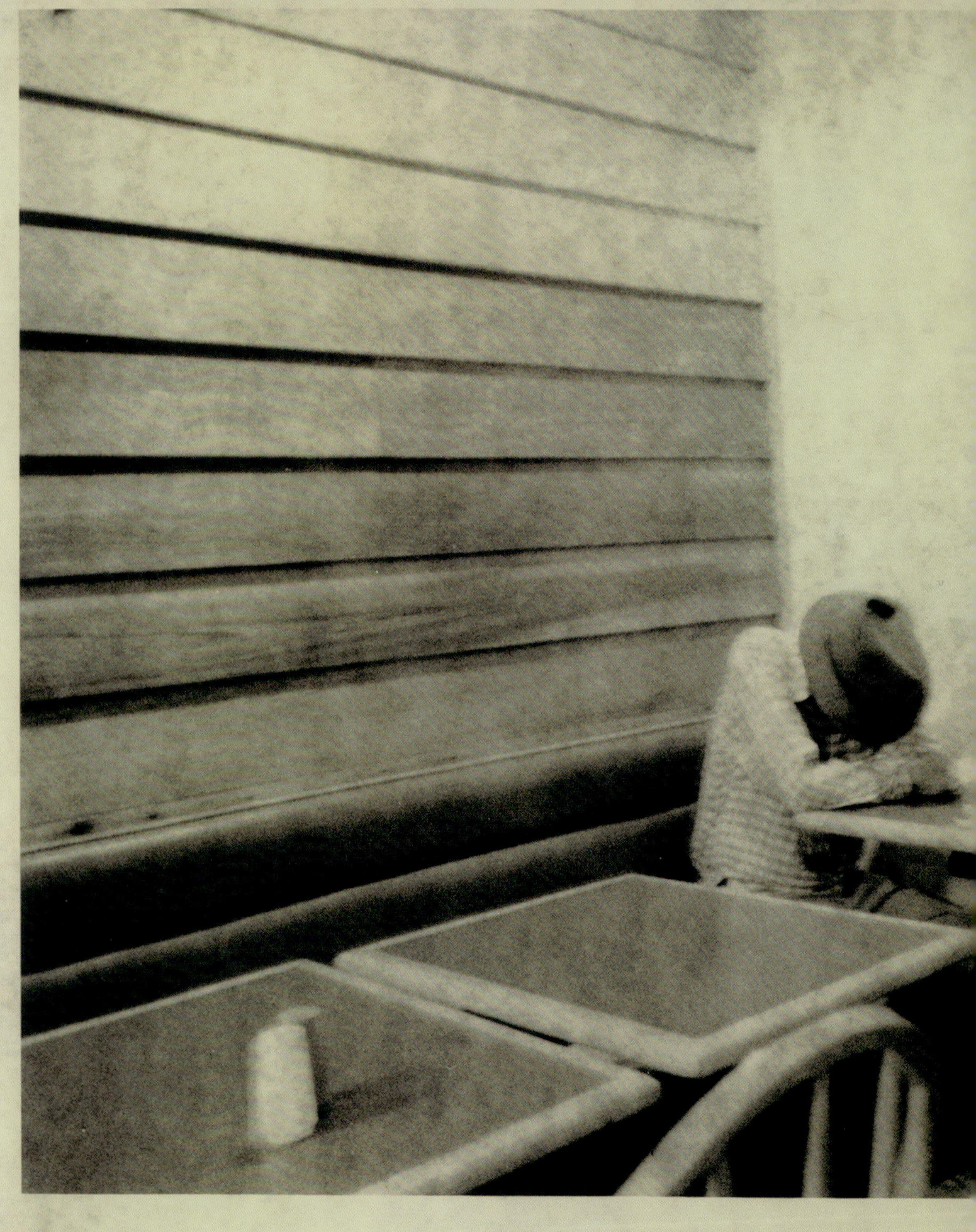

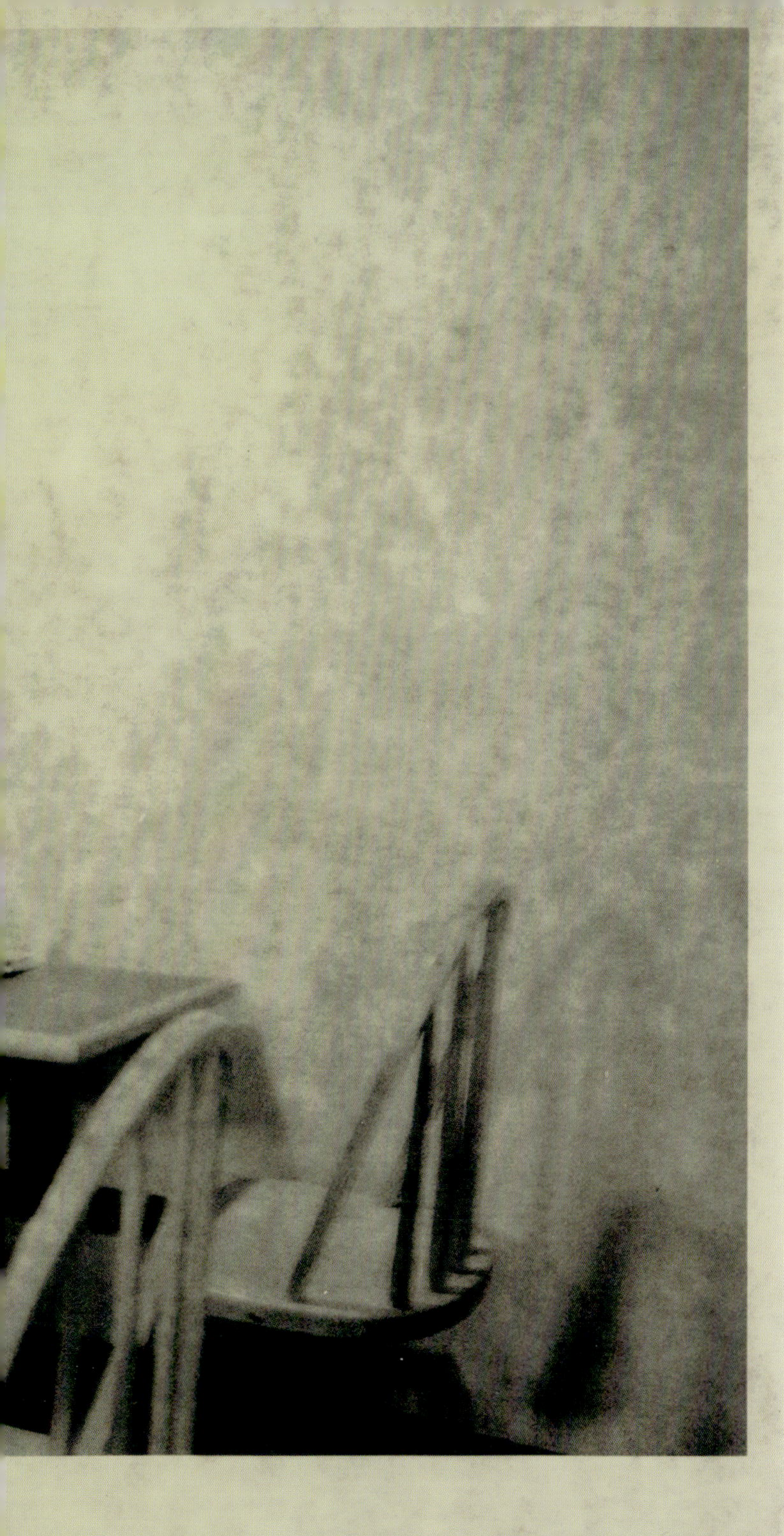

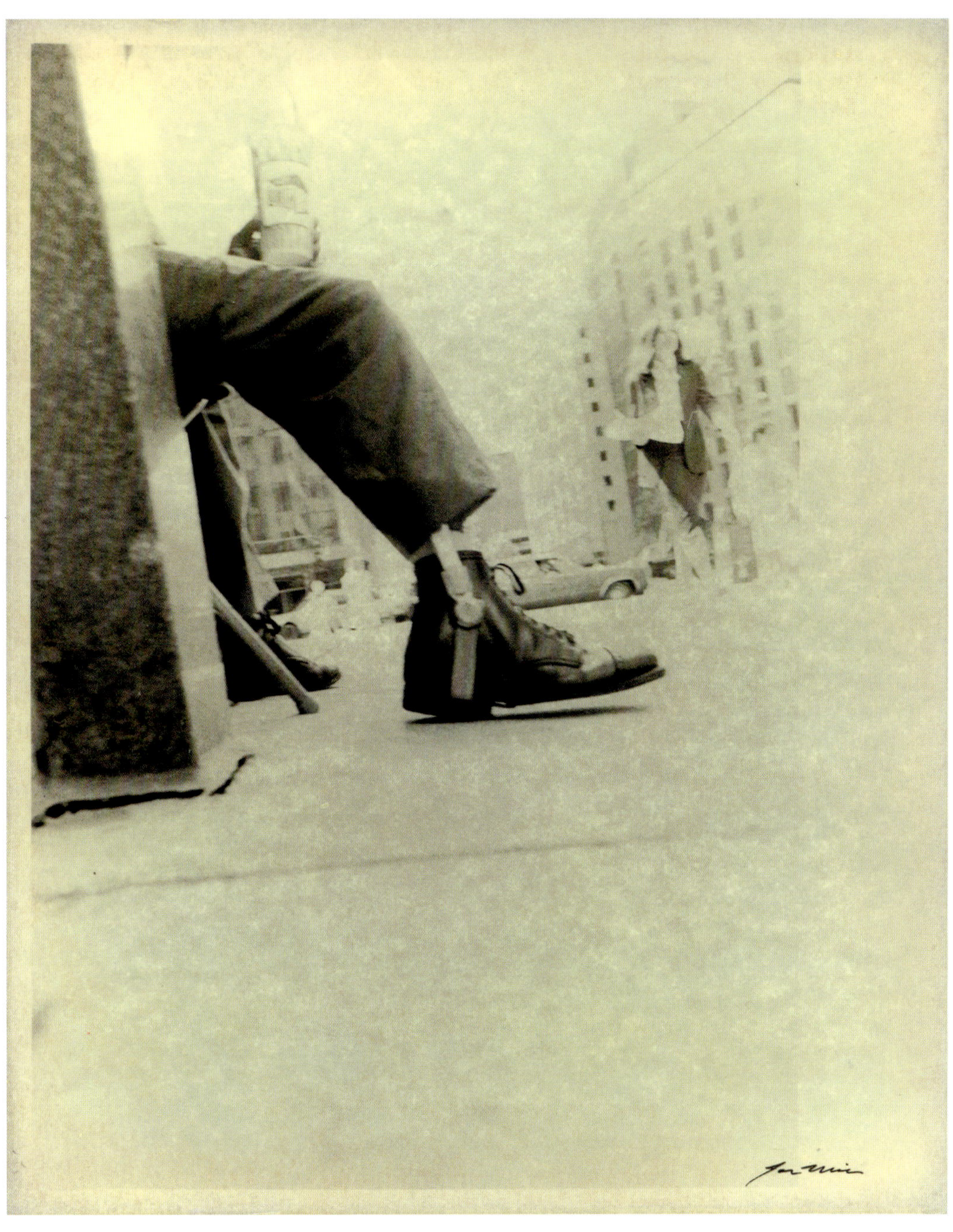

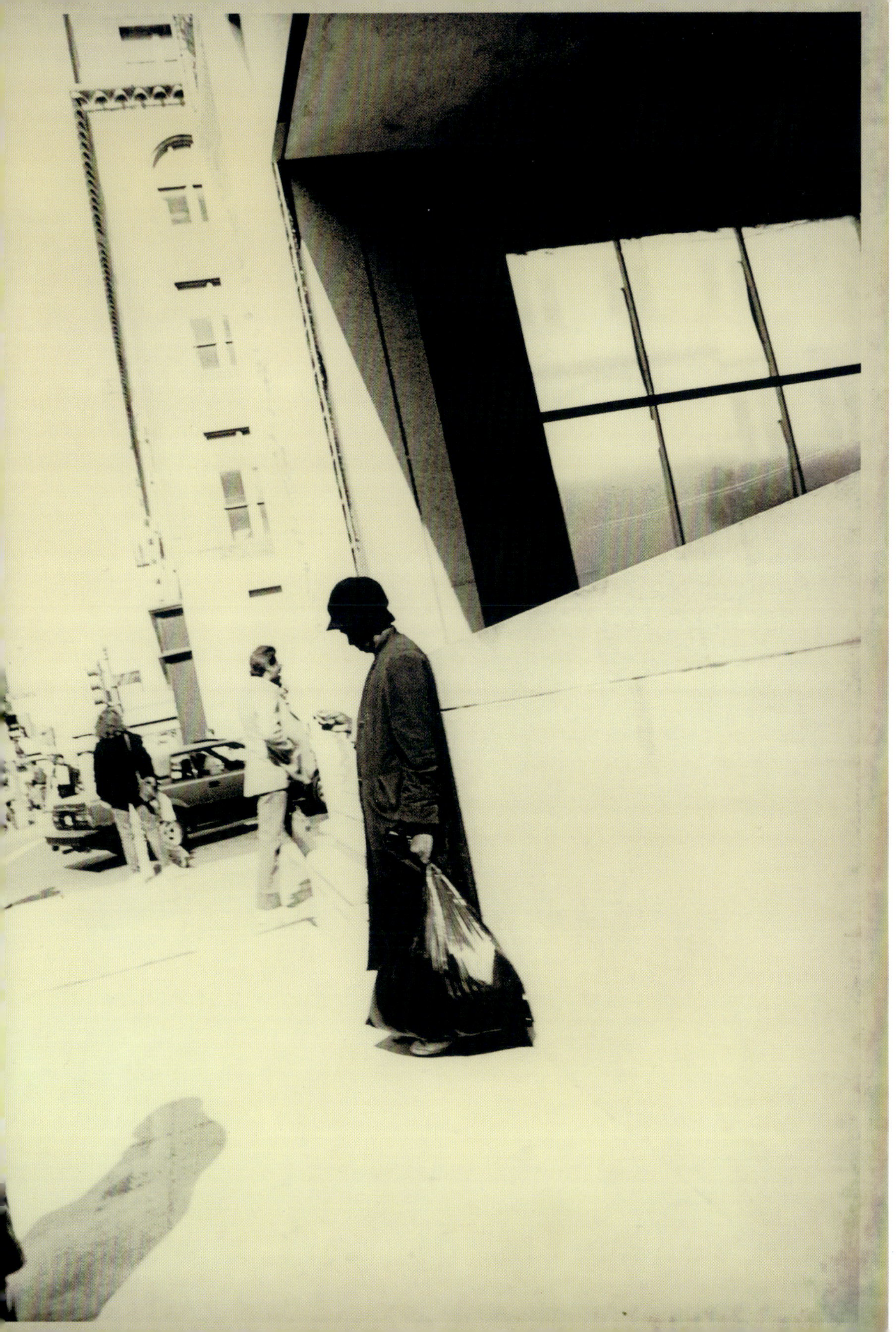

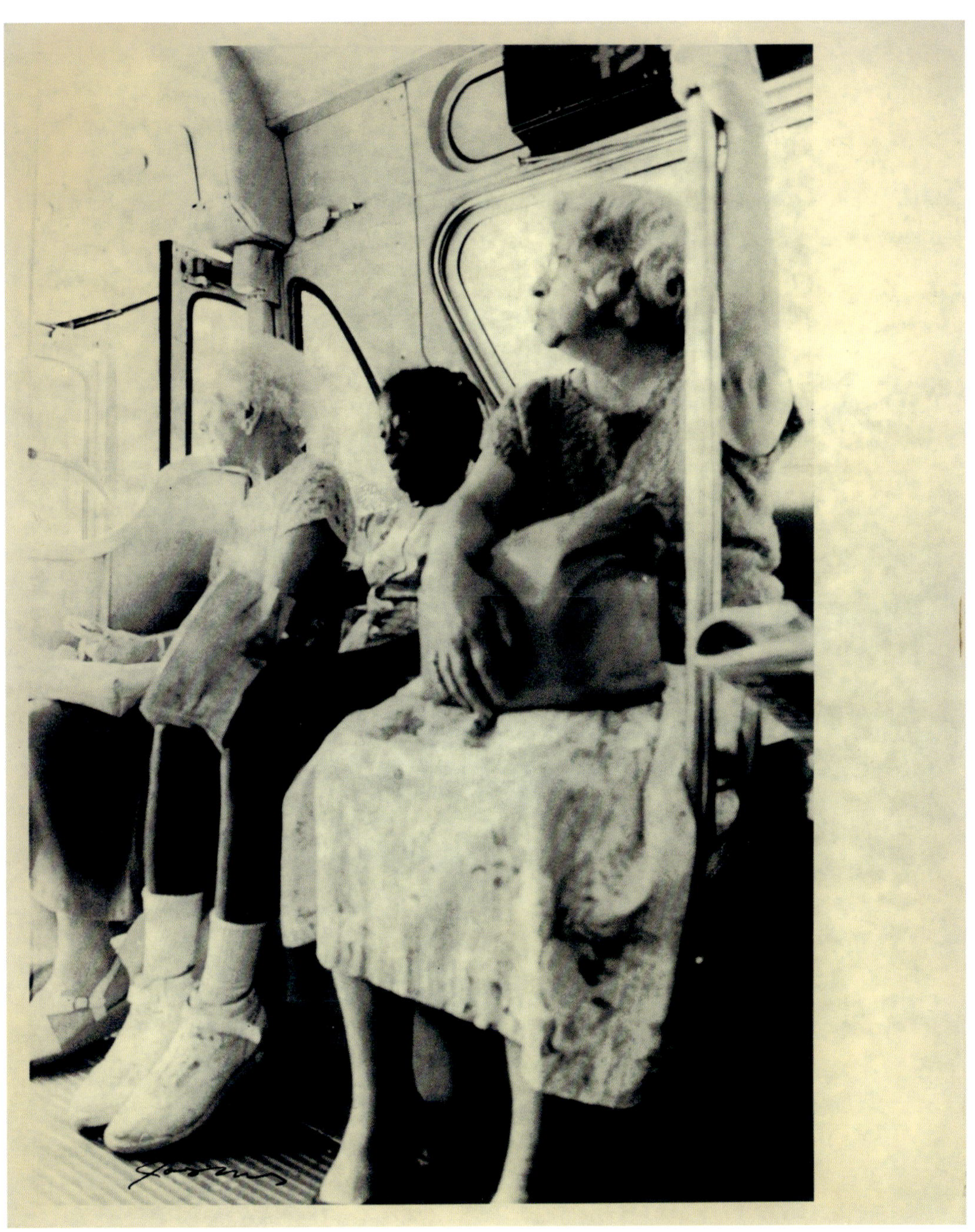

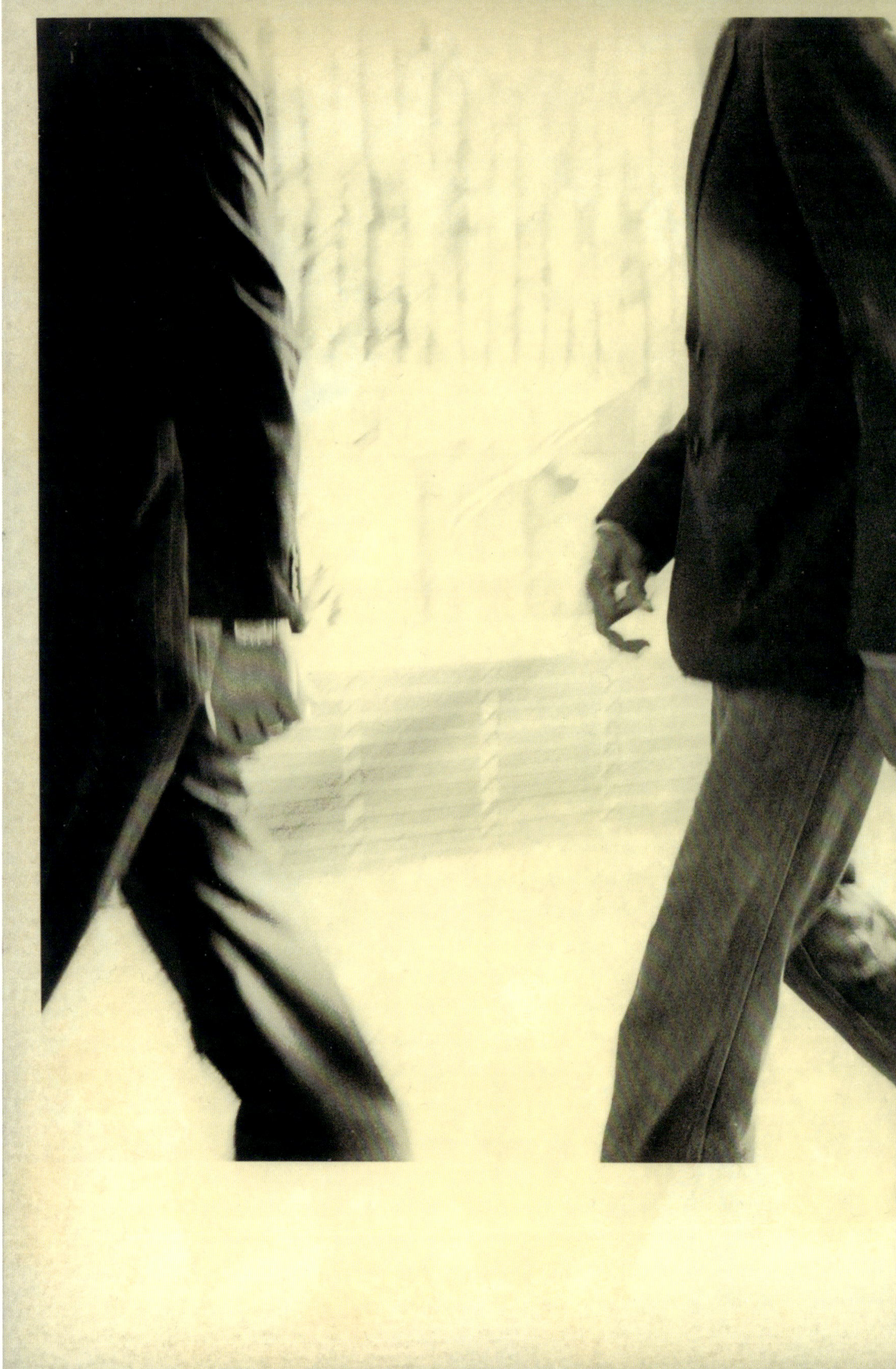

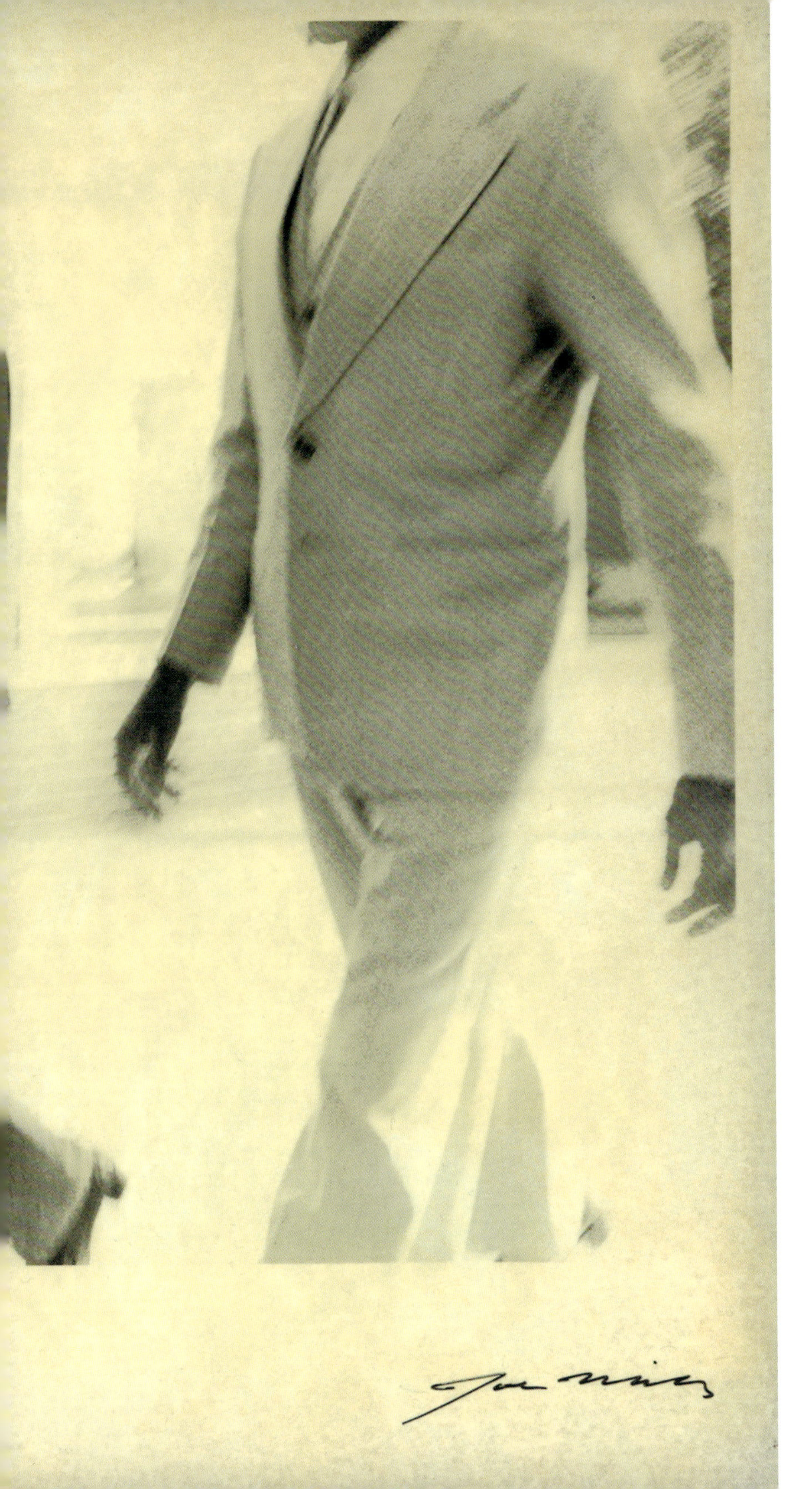

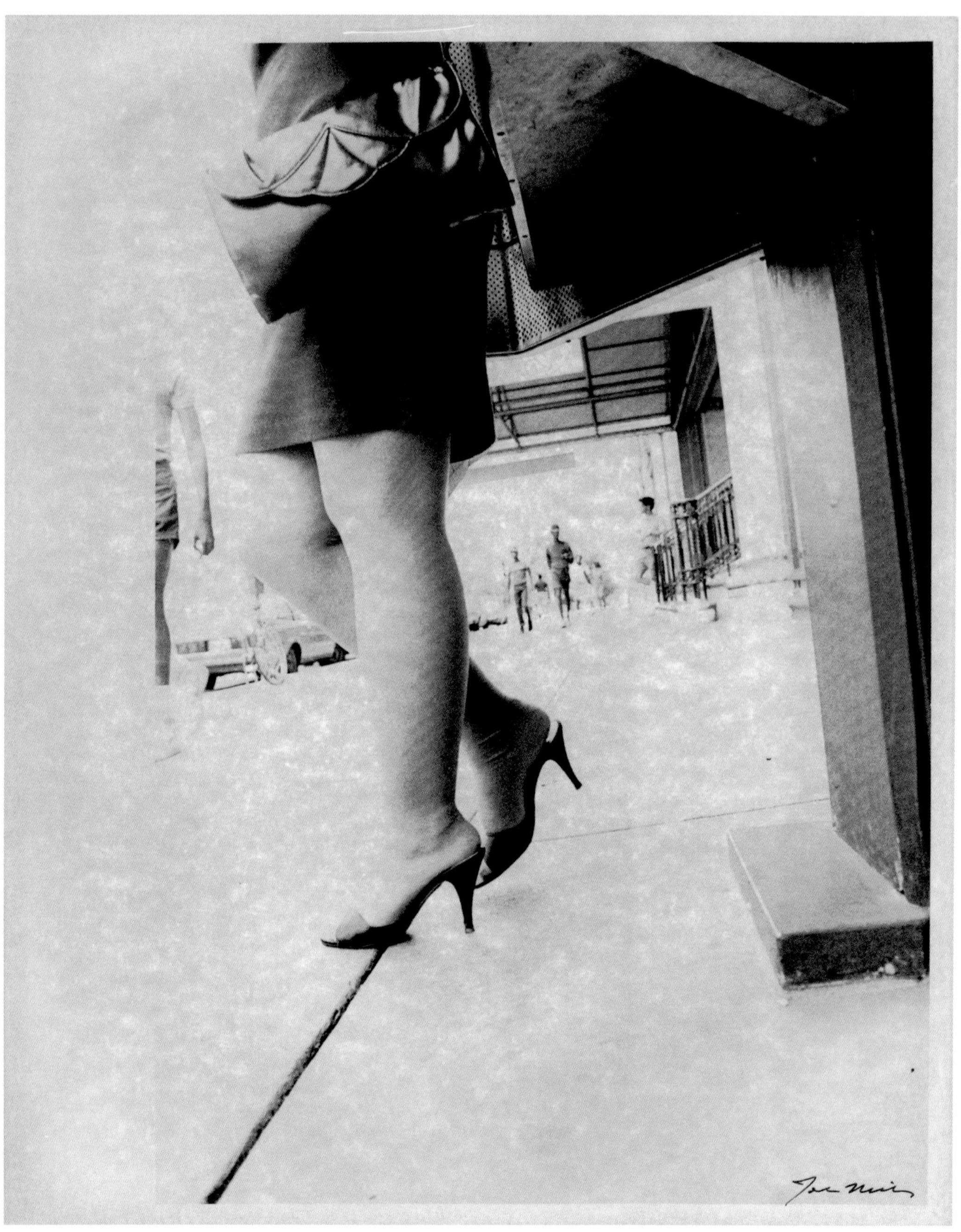

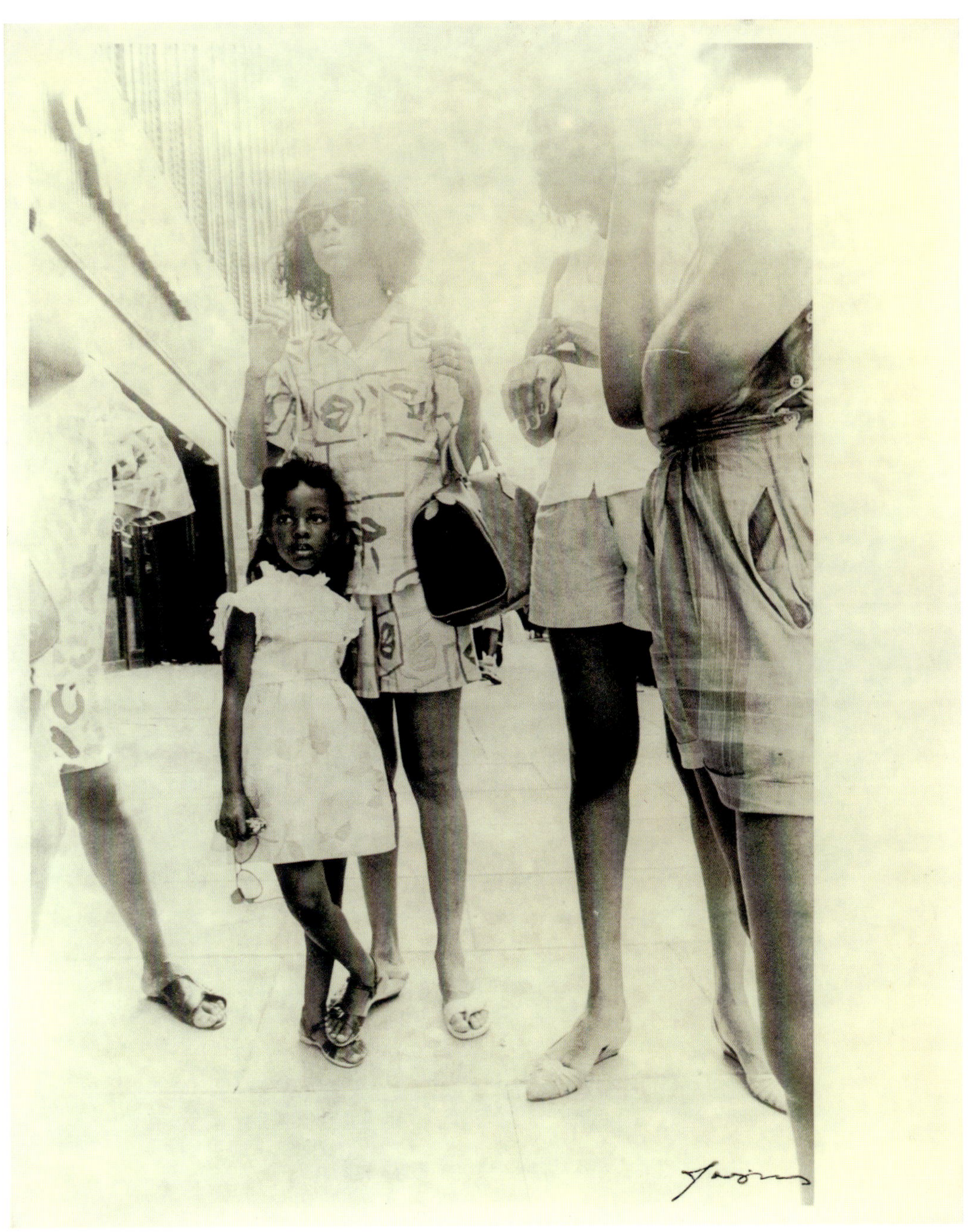

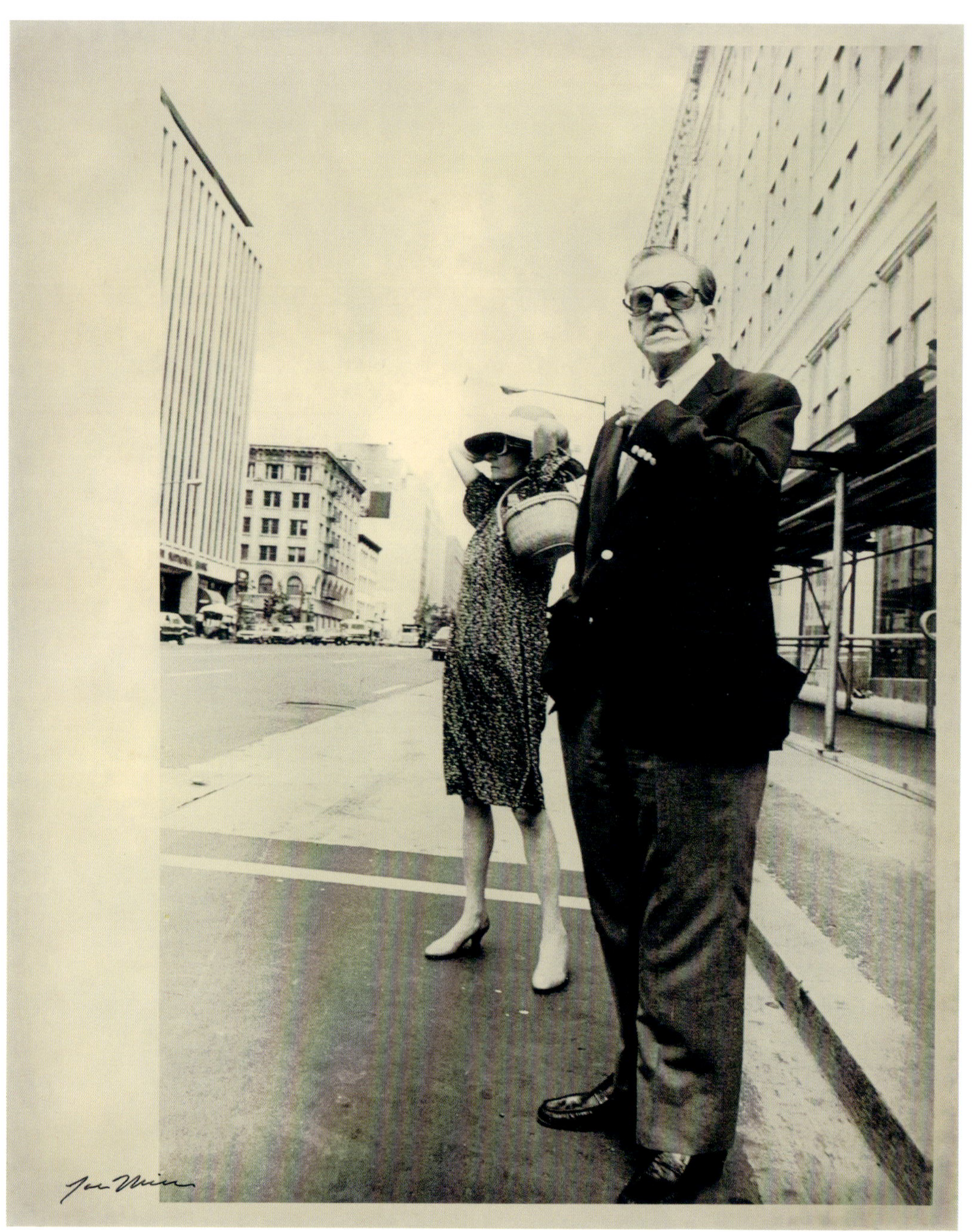

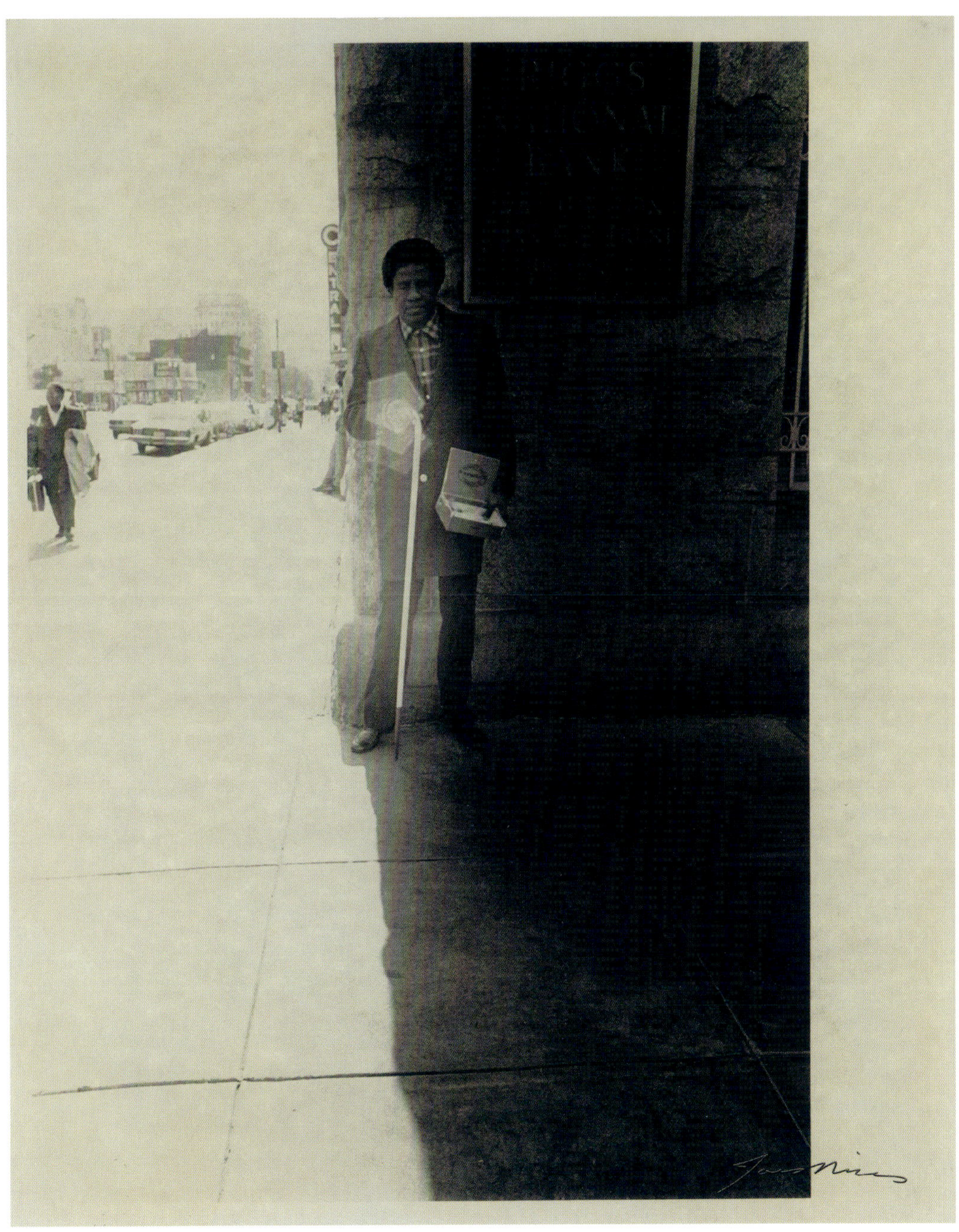
RIGGS
NATIONAL
BANK

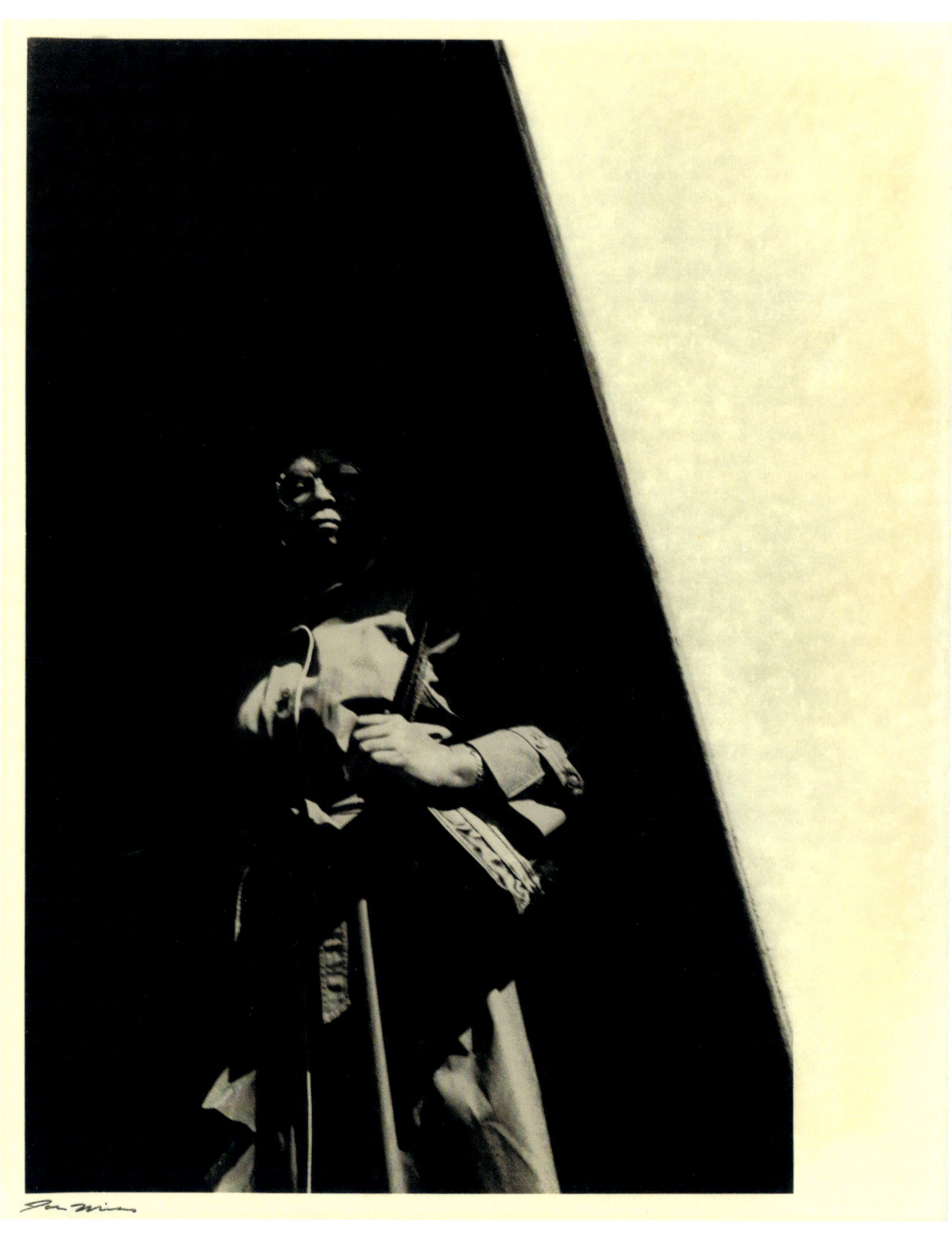

56

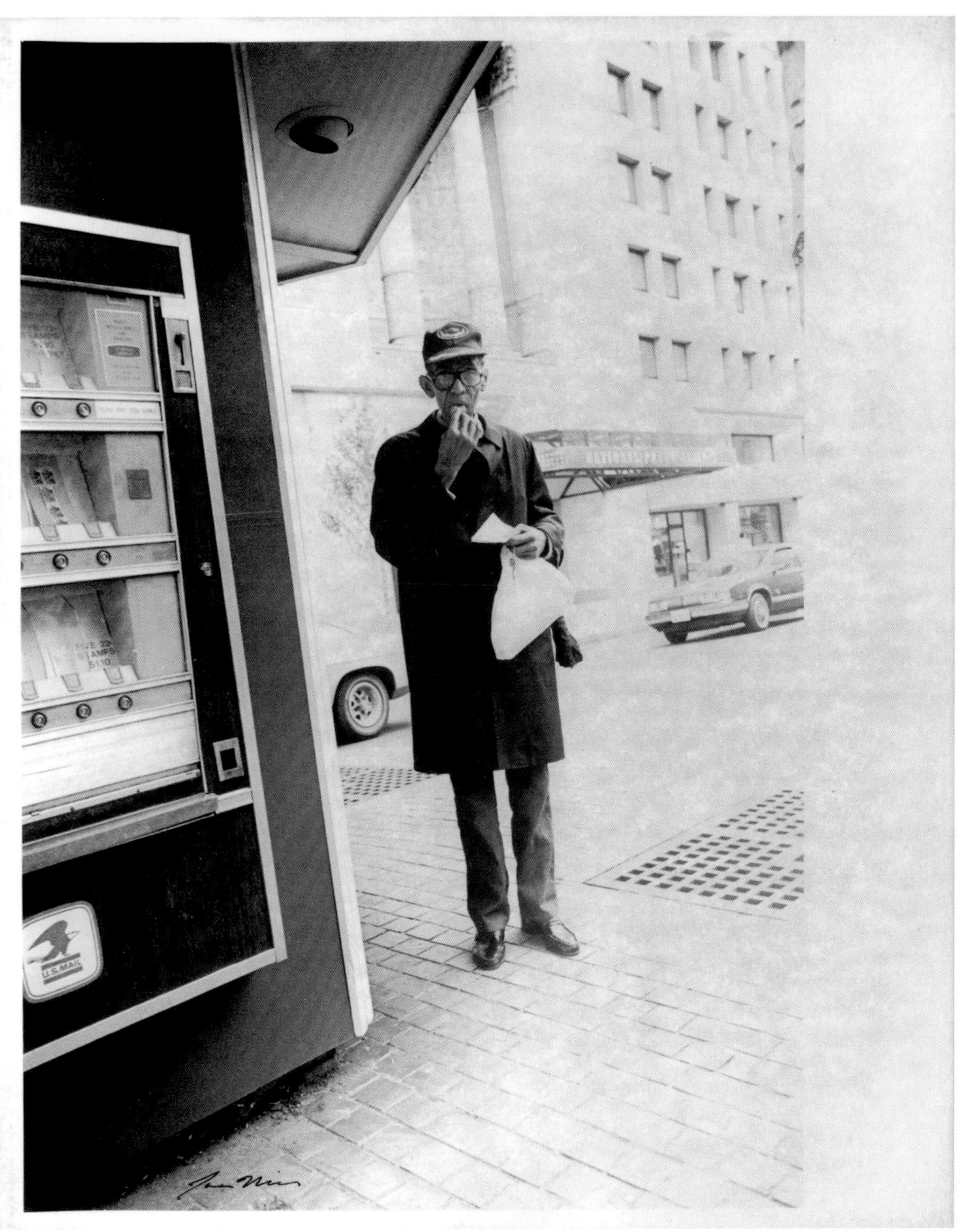
U.S.MAIL

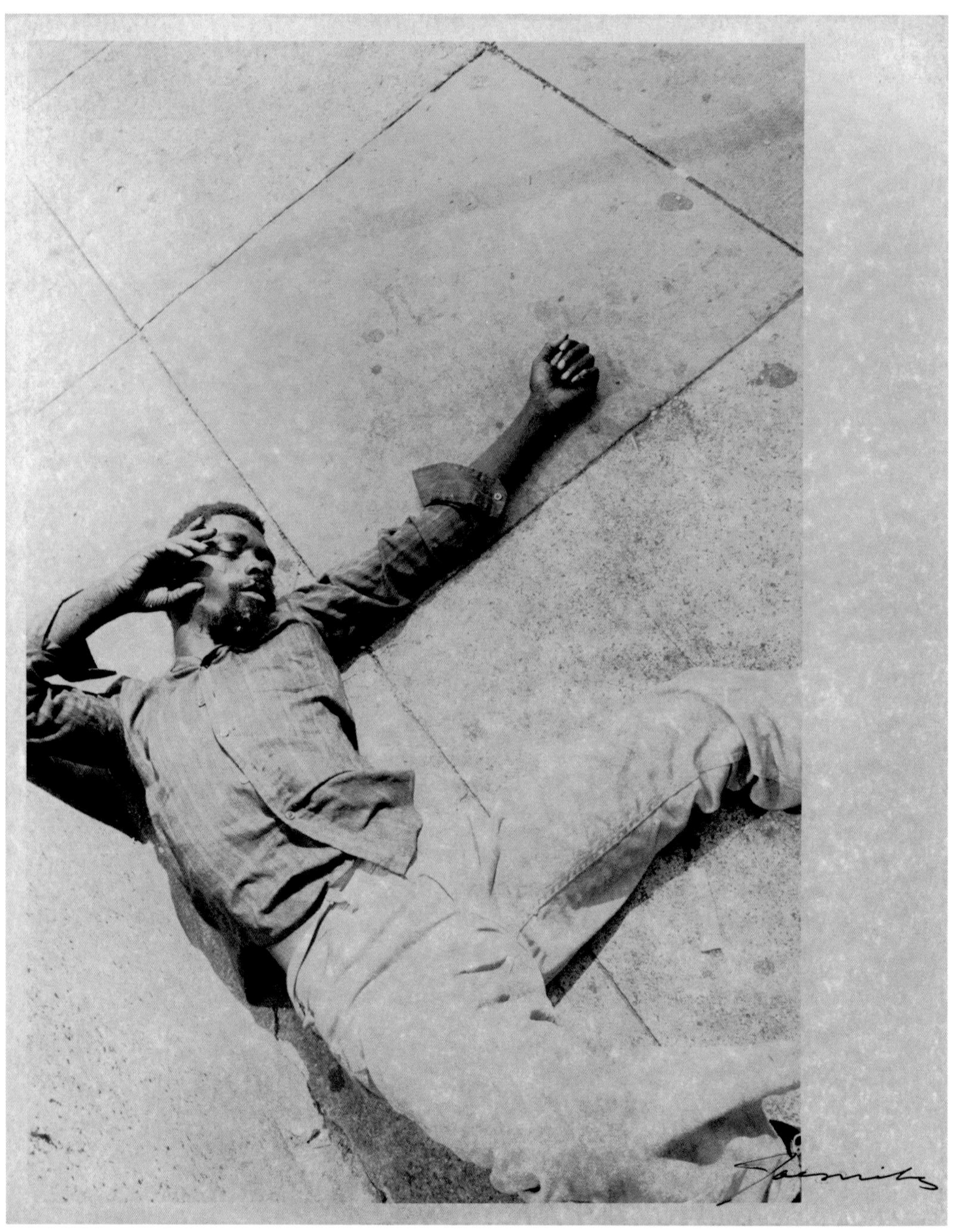

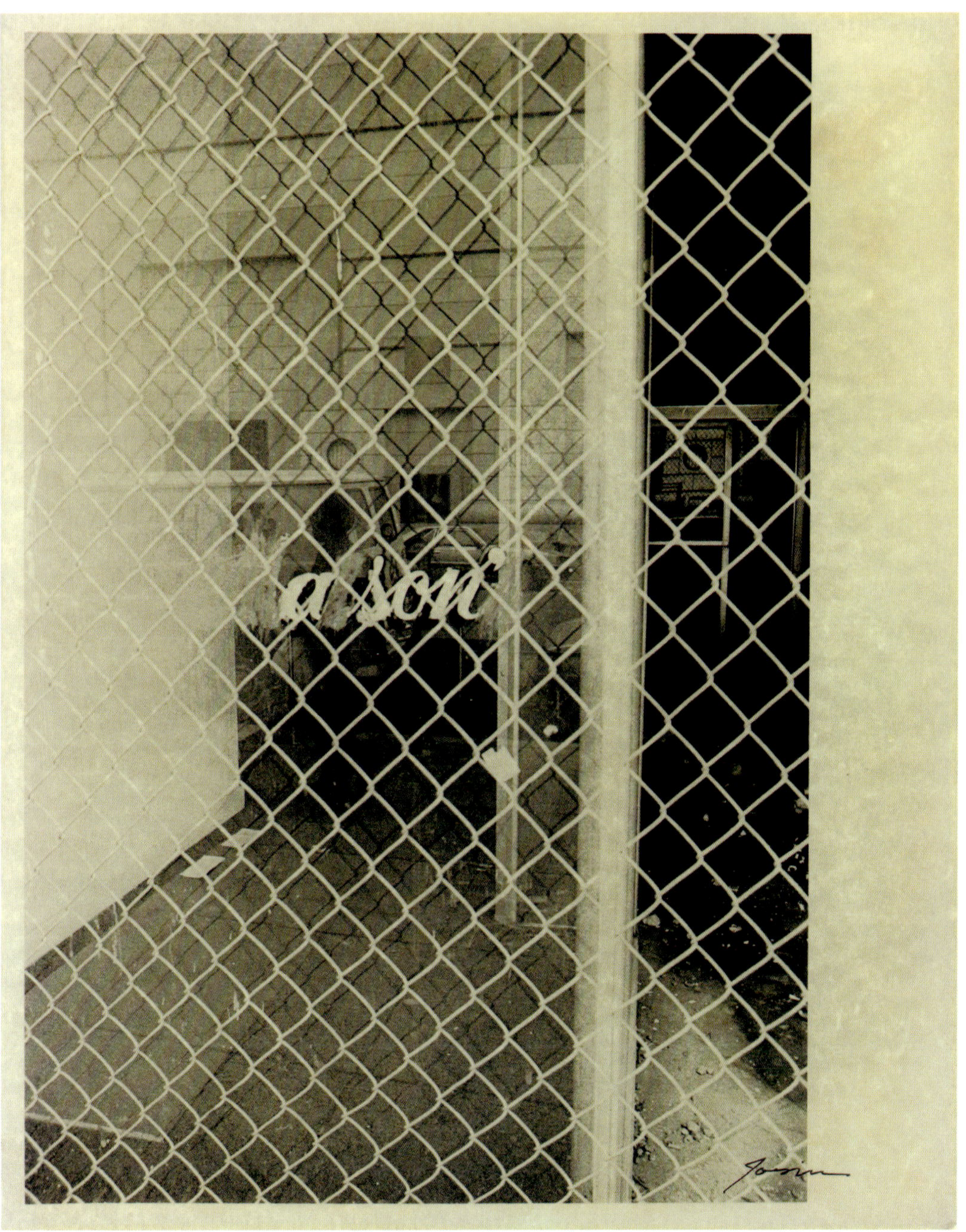
a son'

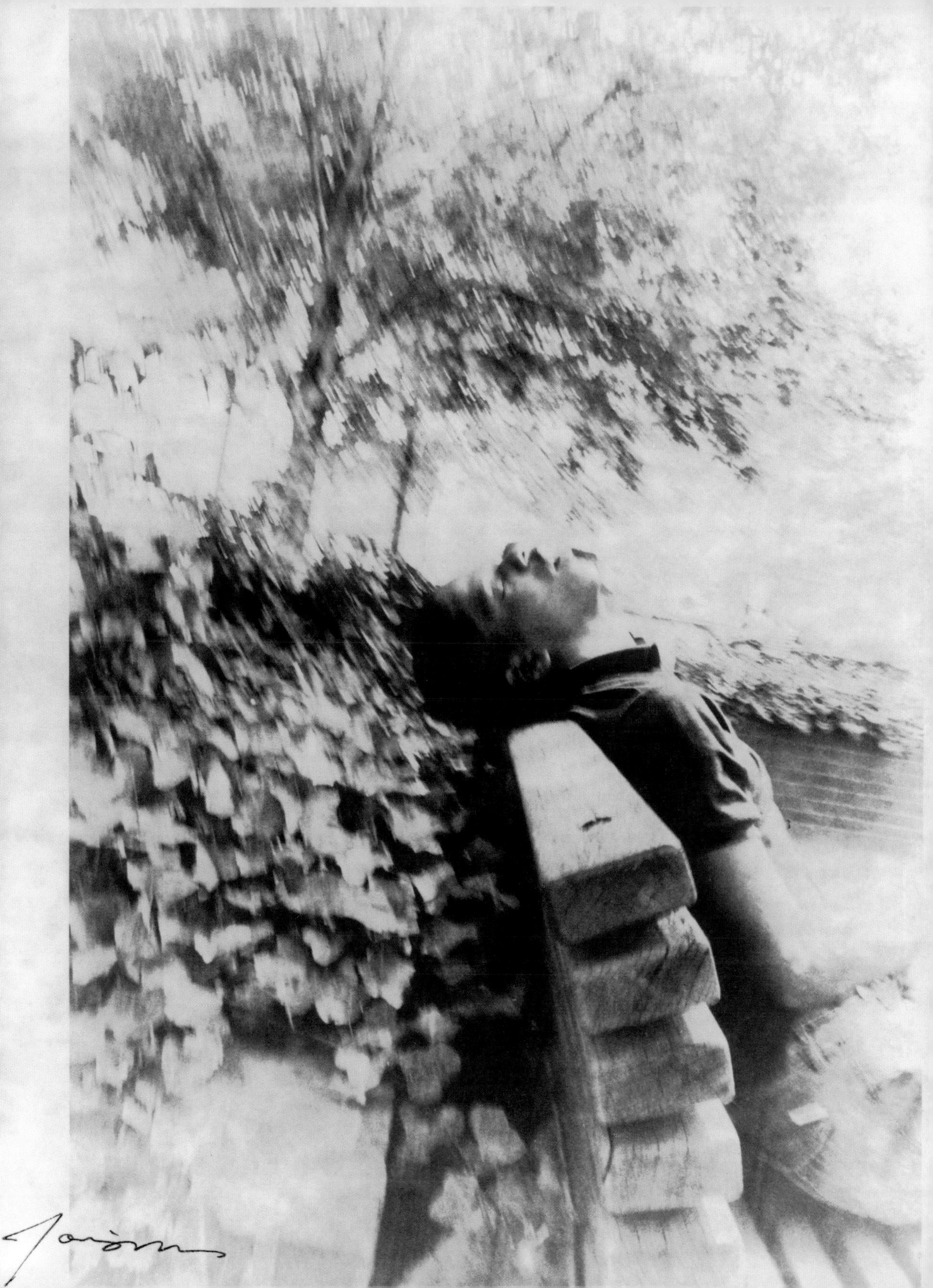

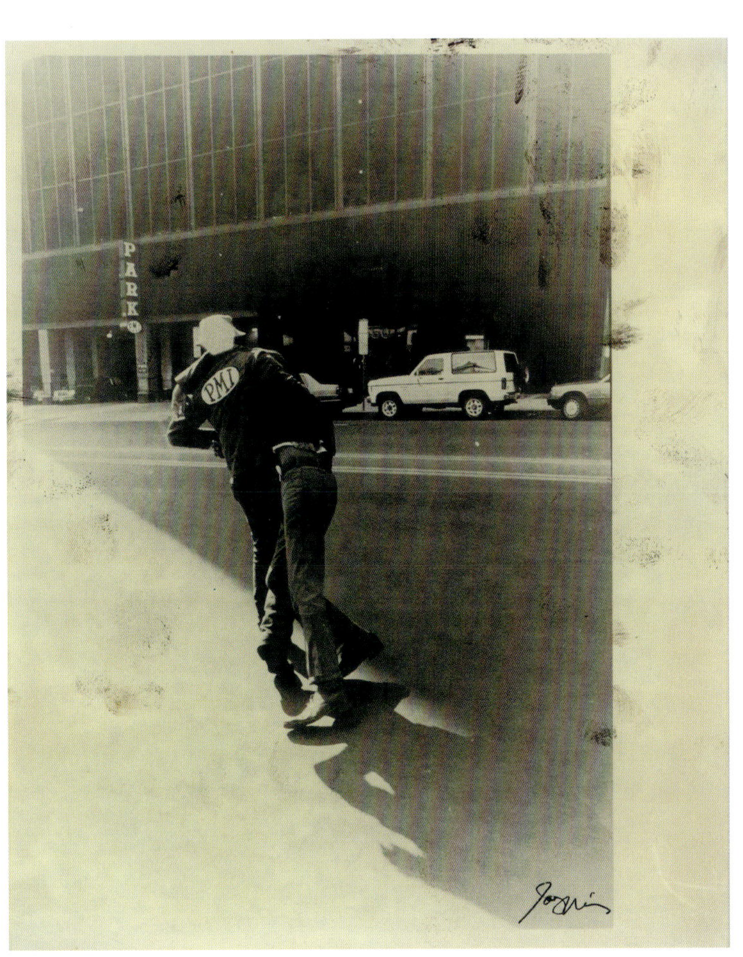

PARK
PMI

On the Edge of Horror and Beauty

Joe Mills' photographs elude my attempts to explain or categorize them. I am seeking words to describe the art of someone whose pictures are intentionally and essentially very difficult to describe. Their meanings rest in spaces that we cannot see, spaces that are created by the tension between the elements that we can describe. In that way, they are closer to poetry than to narrative.

Having photographed since he was 16, and having exhibited and published his photographic art for almost 35 years, Mills is a mid-career artist who has produced three distinct but interlocking series. He is best known for the surreal photomontages and collages.[i] The other two series are the ongoing affair, through photography, with his wife Mary Del Popolo, and black and white street work, out of which *Inner City*, the photographs featured here, was conceived.

The work in this book begins with Mills walking the streets of Washington, DC, with his 35-mm camera. People and their detritus are the focal points of these pictures. His subjects are not Washington's elite, but those whose situations in life are more peripheral and vulnerable. The majority of the images portray children, street prophets, handicapped beggars, amputees, and the homeless as well as those who are mentally unstable or distraught. He also separated out individuals with odd personal quirks, such as a woman temporarily storing her masticated gum on a fingertip, a woman with fingernails as long as her fingers, and a woman inexplicably standing calmly with one foot in a high heel shoe and the other foot bare. While Mills tends to isolate individuals, he occasionally captures pedestrians' interactions, such as one man bumming a cigarette from another or an elderly black man playing shoot-em-up with an Asian child. However, the interactions portrayed are not primarily between people, but between an individual and the hard-cement city with its cacophony of signs, cars, and harshly reflected light.

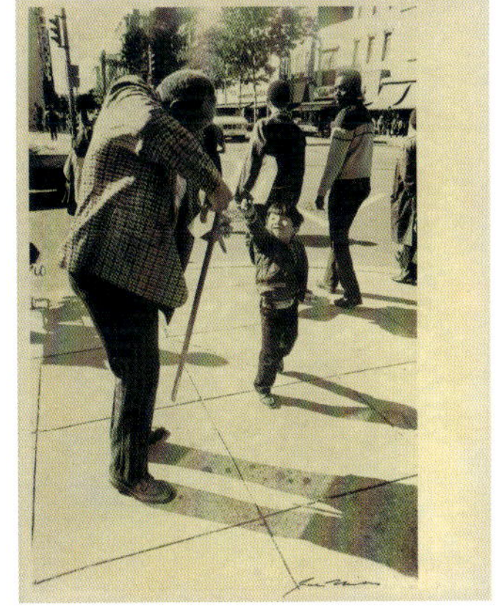

Mills challenged himself to get close, to see plainly and clearly, and not be intimidated by dangers inherent in photographing on the street. He disciplined himself to photograph every summer day over a period of years and, most particularly, to move into those situations that unnerved him. The pictures are both about the inner city life that he records and his own internal conflicts. He said, "I was always out there to discover the line of intimidation within me and to see whether I couldn't step over it."[ii] Mills continued that if he could get past what frightened or repulsed him and get into it, "it would make a good feeling at the end of the day." About each of his series, Mills is plainspoken about wanting to convey what is in his own interior. Ultimately, what unites the seemingly disparate aspects of Mills' work is the quality he admires in the photographs of Robert Frank. "He showed me a way of accepting photography as a strictly personal point of view," wrote Mills, "a photography which is, in the end, simply the expression of what we desire."[iii]

When Mills walked the streets, he often chose to photograph without looking through the camera's viewfinder, expanding considerably the possibilities in both perspective and proximity. Sometimes, Mills took a distant view, and in other moments, he was close enough to have physically touched the subject, who was sometimes only inches away. He might angle the view upward from thigh level or peer straight down a sidewalk from a crouched position, as he did in the photograph with a woman's legs in the foreground. These body fragments in his pictures' foregrounds—a hand, a head, or a shoulder—serve to animate and humanize the surrounding city but leave us with more questions than information. The details that we see are enough to perceive a distinct individual, but too little to form any conclusions about who they are or why they are there. Mills, a skilled picture maker, intrigues us yet keeps us on the edge of unknowing.

With his camera at his side, almost never to his eye, his subjects rarely knew that Mills was taking their pictures. Sometimes there were conversations with them, leading to surprising results. One elderly woman invited him over, pulled on his tie, and slugged him. Other subjects were lost in thought, or sleeping uncomfortably on park benches, against barricades, and even, on the open sidewalks. Sometimes figures are bisected by the sharp light-and-shadow patterns characteristic of cities.

Mills printed the full image of his 35-mm negatives on sheets of 8 x 10 or 11 x 14 inch expired photographic paper, leaving a 1/4 inch border on three sides and a wider border on the fourth—the "well," as he refers to it. Mills then coated the prints with an amber toned varnish. The traditional frame created by the edges of the negative is no longer the sole boundary of what we are meant to see. Rather, the varnish bound the white borders to the elements within the picture. Sometimes the white strips became part of the image, variously extending the dimensions of a street, a sidewalk, or an alley. Consistently, the addition of this space, which is the space where Mills signed his name, undermines the way we traditionally perceive a photograph. The photograph becomes an object, as a painting or a piece of sculpture is an object. There is no longer an illusion of the photograph having sliced a piece of reality out of the flow of life. Mills says that he intentionally "sought something more transitory, something that wasn't about illusion," and in doing so, made "windows onto some world that wasn't really out there."[iv]

Another effect of the varnish is a dreamlike quality that prevails over the specificity of time and place captured in the photograph. The specificity is still there, but the varnish becomes a veil through which we see the subjects and scenes. The resulting images are more open than a documentary photograph to the viewer's own thoughts and interpretations. In the numerous pictures of people sleeping, we become more conscious that they might be dreaming or may even be a dream, our dream. We become conscious of the duality. It is a dream. It is a political/social statement on homelessness. It is both. It is neither…

The varnish is also the unifying link between these street images and Mills' photomontages. Although he made his first collages at age 19, the series truly began in 1983 when he photographed an early collage that was deteriorating in order to preserve the image. Mills liked the way that the process transformed the variegated textures of the collage into the single smooth surface of a piece of photographic paper, both mimicking and, in turn, undermining the traditional straightforward, documentary photograph. This attribute, combined with Mills' superb craftsmanship, convincingly brought the disparate parts of the original collage together. Both Mills' photomontages and the varnished street photographs walk a teetering edge between what is perceived as real and what is a "greater reality."

Speaking of his collage work, Mills described issues also relevant to the street work, *Inner City*:

> I have strong feelings against the de-mystification of my collage work by stressing the techniques that I use. After I take great measures to set up an image, the first thing the viewer wants to do is reassure himself that what is so difficult to look at is not real…. The most accomplished collages exist on the fine line between meaning and mystery. They seem to be on the verge of complete revelation but always leave the viewer on a suspended note. The collage work that I have produced over the past fifteen years has a common thread; the image dares to be understood but stands firm in its refusal to relinquish any part of its meaning in a linear fashion. It remains oblique and functions as a catalyst to stimulate the viewer's own thinking. This is how an image lives.[v]

With the photomontages, Mills uses technique to convince us that the surreal is real, and with the street photographs, Mills uses technique to displace obvious "reality" with a place that seems to originate in his mind, or ours. With the montage work, we, the viewers, may not want the subjects to appear real because the images depict horrific moments. In one, a dog-faced woman kisses an elderly face on a child's body while the "dog" helps the child to dress. In another, a parasite erupts from a man's neck through a cut inflicted while he is shaving. In a third, an angry child rolls his eyes, sticks out his tongue, and forces steam through his ears. Ordinary daily rituals are suddenly transfigured by our worst fears. Reality is out of control. Fears that we usually suppress may not be baseless. The true reality of the pictures is that the created scene evokes an emotional moment to which we connect on our deepest personal levels; however, that moment may remind us of things of which we do not want to be reminded. The success of these images lies in the fact that they are anchored in reality just enough so that we are on

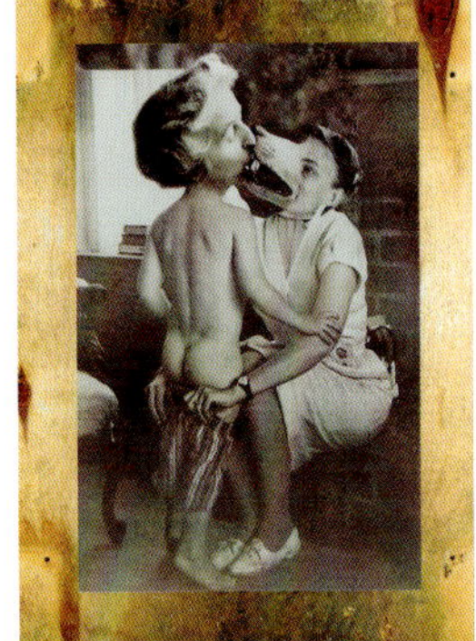

Untitled, 1985, photomontage mounted on found object, and varnished.

the edge between reality and surreality. While we don't want it to be real, it looks so seamlessly real and appealing. The photomontages exist, as does his street work, on the edge of horror and beauty.

Accident is another element shared by the street work and by the photomontage series because Mills builds chance into the process of making both series. Chance is inherently present when working on a city street because people and vehicles converge and collide with no predictable pattern from many directions. To this chaos, Mills removed an element of control by not looking through the camera's viewfinder. In part, he was inspired by the years he spent as a musician and by extemporaneous composition. When editing his contact sheets, he does not look for the "decisive moment," as Henri Cartier-Bresson described that moment when the elements in the picture unite into a formal and narrative epiphany. Mills is more interested in metaphors and in the psychic states stirred within the viewer and within himself.

Mills did not look for pictures, but got into the flow of the street and let the pictures find him. Similarly with the collages, he gathered a wide range of graphics from various sources, letting the images suggest which synthesis would bring a completely new image. He was in control yet relinquished it to trust his intuition. "In any medium I tackled," he said, "I was always looking for something that wasn't in me already."[vi] At least, he was looking for something that he did not know was within him until he found it. As the poet Seamus Heaney once wrote of his own process, Mills goes off to confront his own emptiness. Pushing in the outside leads to the interior unearthings that are in turn put forth for us, the viewers, to make our own discoveries.

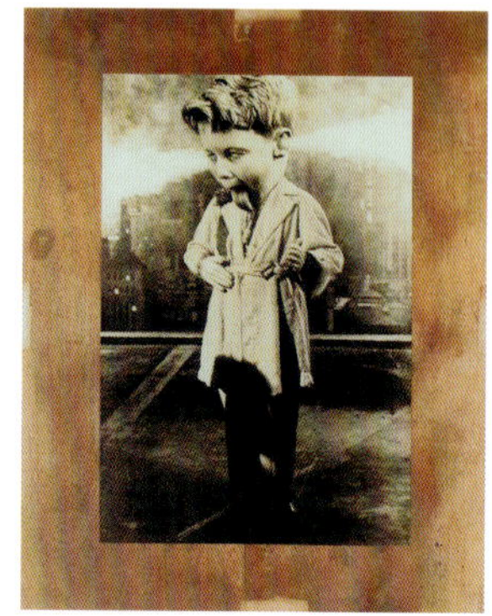

Untitled, 1982, photomontage mounted on found object, amd varnished.

Anne Wilkes Tucker

Gus and Lyndall Wortham Curator
The Museum of Fine Arts, Houston

i A photomontage is a photograph of a collage.

ii Colby Caldwell, "The Unique Vision of Joe Mills," *Washington Review* XXIII:3 (October/November 1997), pg 4.

iii "History of Photography: Influences" unpublished manuscript by Joe Mills.

iv Caldwell, "Unique Vision," pg. 4.

v Joseph Mills, statement in *Un/Common Ground: Virginia Artists 1988* (Richmond: Virginia Museum of Fine Arts, 1988), written and edited by Julia W. Boyd (Richmond: Virginia Museum of Fine Arts, 1988), p. 60.

vi Caldwell, "Unique Vision," pg. 4.

Acknowledgments

Inner City was published through the generous support of Susan Ascher, Phillip Barlow, Norm Carr, Ruth Compton, Evelyn De Boeck, Lisa Gilotty, W.M. Hunt, Melissa Kennedy, Meredith Margolis, Chris Reutershan, and Patricia Smith-Melton.

We would also like to thank the staff at Hemphill; Lisa Bertnick, Christopher Brooks, Mary Early, and Kimberly Gladfelter.

A special thanks goes to Paul Roth, Assistant Curator of Photography and Media Arts, Corcoran Gallery of Art, whose vision was essential in the creation of this publication and the accompanying exhibition.

This book accompanies the exhibition *Joseph Mills: Inner City*, on display at the Corcoran Gallery of Art in Washington, DC from February 15 through April 14, 2003.

The first printing of *Inner City* is limited to 2,000 copies.

Unless otherwise credited, all photographs in this book are part of the series *Inner City* and were shot in Washington, DC between 1982 and 1989. The prints were made on expired photographic paper and varnished.

Book design: Melissa Kennedy
Image selection and sequencing: Melissa Kennedy and Paul Roth
Text editors: Willona Sloan and Lisa Jirousek
Type faces: Oldstyle 7 and STA Portable (Christa Skinner and Edwin Utermohlen)
Paper: Japanese White A

All images are © Joseph Mills.
On the Edge of Horror and Beauty © Anne Tucker
Printed in China © 2003 Hemphill Fine Arts and Joseph Mills.

Nazraeli Press
526 East 16th Street
Tucson, AZ 85701
USA
www.nazraeli.com

Hemphill
1027 33rd Street NW
Washington, DC 20007
USA
www.hemphillfinearts.com

ISBN 1-59005-055-x

Nazraeli Press

HEMPHILL